Creating *and* Sustaining *the* Constructivist Classroom

Second Edition

26.96

To Rachel, who reminds me, in ways both spoken and unsaid, about what is most important in education.

B. M.

To Dave, Jen, Phil, Kachina, and Jeannie, who make it all worthwhile; to Alia, whose smile says it all; and to Gerry, for being there.

M. P.

Creating *and* Sustaining *the* Constructivist Classroom

Second Edition

Bruce A. Marlowe ✤ Marilyn L. Page

CORWIN PRESS
A SAGE Publications Company
Thousand Oaks, California

For information:

Corwin Press
A Sage Publications Company
2455 Teller Road
Thousand Oaks, California 91320
www.corwinpress.com

Sage Publications Ltd.
1 Oliver's Yard
55 City Road
London EC1Y 1SP
United Kingdom

Sage Publications India Pvt. Ltd.
B-42, Panchsheel Enclave
Post Box 4109
New Delhi 110 017 India

Printed in the United States of America

Library of Congress Cataloging-in-Publication Data

Marlowe, Bruce A.
Creating and sustaining the constructivist classroom / Bruce A. Marlowe and Marilyn L. Page.— 2nd ed.
      p. cm.
Includes bibliographical references and index.
ISBN 1-4129-1450-7 (cloth) — ISBN 1-4129-1451-5 (pbk.)
   1. Constructivism (Education) 2. Active learning. 3. Teaching. I. Page, Marilyn L. II. Title.
LB1590.3.M37 2005
370.15′2—dc22

                                                    2004030484

This book is printed on acid-free paper.

05   06   07   08   09   10   9   8   7   6   5   4   3   2   1

Acquisitions editor:	Faye Zucker
Editorial assistant:	Gen Rabanera
Copy editor:	Heather Moore
Typesetter:	C&M Digitals (P) Ltd.
Cover designer:	Lisa Miller
Indexer:	Monica Smersh

Contents

Preface to the Second Edition

Since our first edition (1998) of *Creating and Sustaining the Constructivist Classroom*, the mandates and pressures of the No Child Left Behind (NCLB) Act, in addition to the continued development and implementation of state learning standards and standardized testing, have changed classrooms, teacher behavior, teacher morale, and children's school lives. Teachers are under continuing and growing pressure to teach and assess in particular scripted ways and for particular purposes which may have little or nothing to do with real *learning*. There is nothing new in teachers, parents, government officials, and members of society in general disagreeing over what constitutes *learning* or what constitutes appropriate *assessment and evaluation*. But many teachers have become paralyzed, alienated, confused, lethargic, and/or robotic since the onslaught of these draconian, restrictive, and unsupported mandates. In Chapter 5 of this new edition, we do as we promised in the first edition—we address these two complex issues of understanding and managing the student learning standards and assessing and evaluating student learning in a constructivist classroom. This chapter also includes a special section on *the trouble with rubrics*. Our hope is that Chapter 5 will give teachers the support they need to speak their voices and use approaches to teaching, learning, and assessing that are consistent with what they recognize and understand as *real student learning*.

Where Are We Now?

In general, our purpose in this second edition is the same as the first: We have written this practical guide to constructivism to help pre- and in-service teachers understand the tenets of constructivism more clearly and to implement more easily and effectively constructivist approaches in the classroom, regardless of the external pressures *du jour*. In addition to adding the new and necessary chapter on standards and assessment, we have divided the original chapter on diversity into two, Multiculturalism and Inclusion, to better address the multitude of connected issues. With new readers and all the teachers and principals who have acknowledged the usefulness of our first edition in mind, we have updated every other chapter and added experiences from teachers who have implemented constructivist approaches in the era of standards.

Why Now?

Mounting research, our own experiences as educators, and reports from pre- and in-service teachers support our belief that constructivist, active learning programs are not only more engaging, but promote elaborate knowledge construction; encourage empowered, informed, and independent thinking and doing; foster deeper understanding of concepts; nourish more enduring learning; AND lead to greater command and ownership of content. But even when teachers recognize the value of and want to and try to use constructivist approaches in their classroom, their efforts often produce less than what they expect.

The first problem in trying to implement constructivist approaches is that although constructivist propositions can seem fairly simple, hundreds of observations of, and questions from, pre- and in-service teachers over the past 15 years show that they are not. For example many teachers ask questions such as: What does it mean to have students construct their own knowledge? How is *understanding* different from *recalling?* What does it mean to have students demonstrate their understanding? What does past experience have to do with learning? Does constructivism mean students do what they want? If students are sitting in a circle, does that mean it's constructivist?

The second problem is figuring out how to begin. This translates into questions including the following: How can I change my classroom when there is increased and increasing pressure to conform to top-down mandates? What if the students think constructivist approaches mean they can do what they want? What can I do if the principal and other teachers don't even understand what constructivism means? How can I sustain a vision if the School Board and community do not understand it? What if the school board rewards my principal for encouraging teachers to adopt practices that are not constructivist?

How This Book Is Different From Others

Creating and Sustaining the Constructivist Classroom continues to provide the only *consolidated* discussion on the foundations, research-based results, and practical issues of constructivism. Additionally, our book provides guidelines, practical tips, and models to help both new and experienced teachers to create and sustain a constructivist classroom. We bring together and clarify for educators the theoretical foundations and key issues pre-service and in-service teachers raise about creating and sustaining constructivist classrooms; we give educators the tools to make a mental and practical shift from a traditional to a constructivist format; and we help teachers negotiate the complexities of establishing constructivist classrooms in any school environment, in any grade level, and regardless of whatever new mandate arrives. Checklists will help teachers determine where they are now, where they are going, and how they are doing along the way. Additionally, we include reports on attempts, successes, and problems from teachers at different grade levels and from one special teacher—Susan Jackson.

The Book's Structure

We have, from the beginning, conceived of *Creating and Sustaining the Constructivist Classroom* as a working book; it is designed to be useful, and we expect and hope that copies will be written in and dog-eared. Several of the chapters contain checklists, sidebars, and exercises for student and novice teachers; some of the chapters contain a section we call Tough Questions. These questions are designed to provoke discussion and debate about the challenges and dilemmas active learning environments pose for pre- and in-service teachers and education professors.

As in the first edition of this book, we begin with a cautionary tale about the dangers of trying to do too much too soon. In Chapter 1, you will meet Susan Jackson, a beginning teacher with big ideas and big problems. Chapter 2 provides a definition, and explains the historical roots, of contemporary constructivism; additionally Chapter 2 looks at how early active learning movements have come of age. Chapter 3 provides the research-based rationale for creating the constructivist classroom and reviews and summarizes the learning standards recommended by the professional teacher organizations: NCTM, NSTA, NCTE, and NCSS. The fourth chapter challenges and allows teachers to self-assess by reflecting on current practice with regard to the use of language, student teacher roles, classroom management, the classroom communication system, and understanding of motivation. These self-assessments lay the groundwork for creating a constructivist classroom.

New to this edition is Chapter 5, which focuses on the extent to which current reform efforts, particularly those concerned with standards and assessment, are or are not consistent with constructivism. Look for the special section on Rubrics. Chapter 6 provides suggestions for preparing students, parents, and administrators for classroom changes and then introduces and defines four specific, practical active learning models ready for implementation. In Chapter 7, teachers and students in different academic levels describe their experiences with creating, sustaining, and/or succeeding in, constructivist classrooms.

The next three chapters address special issues. In Chapter 8, Technology, we explore the potential of technologically supported and driven schools and classrooms and also provide a framework for integrating current and future technologies to enhance student learning. Chapter 9, Multiculturalism, raises and addresses the challenges connected to working in classrooms that include new immigrant and refugee groups and the increasing number of students who live in poverty. Chapter 10, Inclusion, offers practical guidelines and tips for understanding and working with the issues that arise in mixed ability classrooms.

We return in Chapter 11, the Epilogue, to the beginning—for an update on Susan—and then turn to the future for your journey.

About the Authors

Bruce Marlowe is the editor (with Alan Canestrari) of *Educational Foundations: An Anthology of Critical Readings* (SAGE Publications). He earned his Ph.D. in Educational Psychology from the Catholic University of America in Washington, D.C., where he also completed two years of post-doctoral training in neuropsychological assessment. He has taught at the elementary, secondary, and university levels and is currently Associate Professor of Educational Psychology and Special Education at Roger Williams University. He lives in Rhode Island with his wife and daughter.

Marilyn Page is graduate faculty in Curriculum and Instruction at The Pennsylvania State University. She began her career in education as a high school social studies teacher and has taught in every grade from 7th to 12th, at every academic level, in rural, suburban, and urban school systems. She received her Ed.D. from the University of Massachusetts in Amherst in Instructional Leadership: Secondary Teacher Education and in Educational Media and Instructional Technology. She is currently Technology Coordinator for the Social Studies Teacher Education Programs at the Pennsylvania State University. She consults on novice teacher issues, reform issues, social studies education, and technology in education. She lives in State College, Pennsylvania.

The Novice Teacher: Armed and Dangerous

A Cautionary Tale

As professors whose primary experience at the college level has been in teacher education programs, we have had the opportunity to teach and learn with hundreds of prospective teachers. Many leave their training with an almost palpable zeal for change. Unfortunately, enthusiasm, strong teaching skills, and even a love for students and learning are not enough. Making change, any change, is slow, sometimes painful, and exponentially more difficult as the number of people one wants to include in the change process increases—which is why we begin this book with a cautionary tale about the peril of banking on achieving too much too soon.

Susan Jackson

One of our best students, a young woman we'll call Susan Jackson, was as excited about teaching as anyone we can remember. Susan was a crackerjack student. She was dynamic, engaging, and highly inquisitive. She was interested not only in how things worked in educational settings but also in why the pieces fit together the way they did. Her curiosity was contagious. In fact, of all the students we have known, Susan stood out in terms of both her intellectual curiosity and her enthusiasm—enviable traits for a teacher charged with actively engaging students in learning. Susan also was among the very strongest students we had in terms of her ability to grasp theoretical issues, articulate her arguments, and integrate theory with practice. Finally, she had excellent writing and verbal communication skills, and by the time she graduated, Susan had accumulated a solid repertoire of very creative ideas about how to help students develop these important skills. In short, Susan represented the best our system has to offer, and in many ways she seemed like a perfect candidate for becoming a strong change agent as well.

Susan's story is a common one. Armed, ready, and excited for constructivist teaching, she found herself surrounded by teachers who simply did not see things her way and students unprepared to play along—but we're getting ahead of ourselves. Let's start at the beginning with Susan's culminating college experience of working in a ninth-grade English classroom. Here is what Susan had to say about what her "dream school" would look like shortly before her culminating project began.

Susan's Ideal World

In my ideal world, I will graduate and get a well-paying, teaching job at a progressive school where the students and teachers are self-motivated—where teachers, administrators, and students work together to create exciting, fascinating, fun learning experiences. The best part of working in my dream school, though, is that it is filled with problem solving yes-sayers rather than griping nay-sayers. When an exciting or unusual opportunity for teaming presents itself, the members of my school community will get together and say, "We really must find a way to make this happen," rather than, "Oh, we couldn't possibly do that because . . ." In addition, I want to be in a school just to be in a school. I want to sit at a lunch table with good teachers who care about their students and just listen to what they have to say. I want to be in a place where I can ask more than one teacher, "This is what happened to me today. What would you do in this situation?" I want to see for myself what it is like to have 5 special-needs students in a class of 20. I want to hear the kinds of things that teachers gripe about in low voices during free periods in the day.

Susan's Experience at the High School

As Susan would later discover, high school freshmen, classrooms, and schools are often significantly shy of her dream. Nevertheless, Susan had the good fortune of working with a teacher who was open to new ideas, ready for some experimentation, and willing to follow her lead for at least one major project. The excerpt below comes from Susan's self-evaluation of her culminating experience.

One of the first questions I asked Marcia (the cooperating teacher) was, "How much freedom do we have in terms of what the students can explore, how they go about doing it, and how they show us what they have learned?" She explained that the school had already decided that all 9th grade students would do a unit on Greek mythology. She said that this had been the case for several years. She explained the ways in which she had taught the topic in the past but said that she was willing to try a new approach. From what I gathered, her approach in the past was fairly "traditional." As I understood it, she had the class begin with the Greek story of the creation of the earth, which the whole class read and discussed together. She then had them move into the hero stories and then moved on to several of the other well-known myths. She said that in the past she gave weekly quizzes on vocabulary and content and ended the unit with a comprehensive exam. In other words, Marcia's approach in the past had been to try to expose each student to several (and all the same) of the Greek myths and to discuss some of the broad themes like the role of the hero in Greek mythology.

The approach I advocated was a bit different. The model I used was basically the model used in many of my college classes. I suggested that each student either alone or with a partner, pick a myth, a mythological character, or some other aspect of Greek culture and create an original exhibition to present to the class. Using this approach, each student would have the opportunity to become an expert on some aspect of Greek culture or mythology and, because they had to present to the entire class, all of the students would be exposed to every topic. Marcia said that she liked the idea of projects, although she also said that she had never given the students total freedom in choosing the topics, and she was interested to see how well they would handle it.

For my first lesson, I introduced myself, told them a bit about my philosophy of learning, and explained to the class that I needed their help. I needed to know what they thought were the qualities of a good teacher. We spent the rest of the period generating this list. For their homework assignment, Marcia asked the students to pick the two or three qualities they thought were most important and to explain why these qualities were at the top of their personal lists. In addition, I asked the students to write me a short letter that began, "Dear Miss Jackson, one thing I liked about today's class was that . . . and one thing I did not like or did not understand about today's class was that . . ." The letters were a wonderful way to begin to get to know the students. I could also begin to identify which students were willing to take some time to think about the question and which students just wrote something down to get it over with.

The next step in this process was to try to determine what the students already knew about the Greeks and Greek mythology. In addition, I wanted the students to begin thinking about ways they could demonstrate their understanding of a topic other than by taking a test or writing an essay. We spent the last half of the class talking about what authentic assessment means. We generated another list, similar to the good teacher list, and I gave each student a copy. Following these discussions I struggled with the following questions:

How do I get them to understand what a great project looks like?

What would be a good way to have students tell me what they are thinking of exploring for their exhibitions?

How will I know if my expectations are clear?

How can I make sure that the students are actually doing something productive and moving forward, and not just goofing off in the library?

I came up with the idea of an update sheet. I asked the students to fill out an update sheet during the last few minutes of each class period. I intended to look over the sheets at the end of each day to try to assess where each student was in the process and to help me pinpoint students who might need my help finding resources. Approximately two weeks into the project, I asked the students to fill out a final contract telling me exactly what they had planned to do for their exhibitions. I also gave the students a document that explained the criteria (which they helped develop) on which they would be evaluated. Attached to the evaluation sheet was a calendar which showed the students which days they were scheduled to present.

Overall, the presentations went well. Many of the students' exhibitions were exceptional. Some of the students made video- and audiotapes. Others wrote and performed original monologues in costume. One student made an incredibly lifelike clay sculpture of Hercules slaying the Hydra. After the student's presentation, the principal asked if he could display the statue in the center of the front hall. Two students even researched the eating habits of the ancient Greeks and cooked an ancient Greek feast for the entire class. While we ate, our chefs used a map they had created to explain the ancient Greeks' trade routes and the origins of the products they bartered.

Preparing for the Real World

Susan's experience was, in many ways, both transformative and validating. She had learned about constructivist approaches in her college classes and had a positive and successful experience trying them out. As she prepared for her first full-time teaching job in the Northeast, where she was hired as a member of a middle school team specifically to nudge some of the older teachers toward more progressive practice, the following questions that she created as part of her culminating college experience guided her:

- *How can I facilitate students' learning in such a way that I provide opportunities for them to discover, create, and apply knowledge for themselves while working within a public school setting?*
- *How can I get students to push themselves beyond what they dreamed they were capable of?*
- *How can I get them to want to truly understand what they learn and to demonstrate that understanding in a meaningful and creative way, rather than just memorizing information and spitting it back out on a test?*
- *How do I get students to understand that learning for learning's sake is cool and fun, and hard, and much more worthwhile than memorizing information for a grade and then forgetting it?*

The Reality and the Poem

These are tough questions, but Susan, buoyed by her successful culminating experience, a long summer break, and the confidence of a much more experienced teacher, felt ready to tackle them head-on. What she found when she arrived was anything but what she expected.

By October of her first year of teaching, six short weeks into the semester, Susan sent us the following poem.

I Hate—A Poem by a First-Year Teacher

I hate preparing lessons.

I hate that feeling of panic of "what am I going to do tomorrow?"

I hate vomiting in the morning.

I hate kids who try to slime out of doing things like Steve and Billy do.

I hate getting up at five o'clock (or four-forty-five, or four-thirty).

I hate it when Pamela reminds me of Stacy Jefferson, the girl who made my life hell in seventh grade.

I hate it when Elizabeth Milios yells at a kid who is crying because he is having problems with his ex-girlfriend.

I hate it when Cindy Tuppan looks at me with that bitchy smirk and I know she would secretly love to see me fail.

I hate territorial teachers.

I hate feeling incompetent.

I hate crying when I feel like this.

I hate not having any friends here.

I hate feeling lost.

I hate it when a 14-year-old can make me feel exactly the way I felt when I was 14 years old.

I hate it when kids talk when I am trying to tell them something.

I hate it more when kids who were talking ask me, "Now what are we supposed to do?"

I hate Fridays because that means Monday is only three days away.

I hate Sundays because that means Monday is tomorrow.

What happened? Could this be the same Susan Jackson who left our program so confident, determined, and excited about teaching? By November things had not improved. Another letter, this one more urgent, followed:

Last Monday was definitely the lowest point in my life. We had a great in-service. We had to sit at tables with our teammates and the workshop leader told us all about the kinds of things that he has done with interdisciplinary units, and he showed us how to start with a topic that middle school kids are interested in and then make a web of related topics, etc. Things were going well, overall. After lunch, we met with him as grade-level teachers for about an hour and he asked us to voice concerns that we had with our particular students. It was then that I realized how little faith the teachers at this school have in the students at our school. They truly don't believe that the kids have any desire to learn. They really believe that the kids have to be bribed to do anything.

So after we met with the workshop leader, we were supposed to go upstairs as a team and brainstorm ideas about ways we might be able to do an interdisciplinary unit our-selves. So . . . I got upstairs and John (the social studies teacher who only lectures and teaches straight out of the social studies textbook) was sitting at his desk, and I said, "So do you want to meet in here?" At the same moment, Cindy Tuppan (a science teacher) walked in and John said, "Yeah—whatever. Do we even need to meet? What's the point? I'll tell you what we could do. We could just sit here and pretend to be meeting in case Mr. Schwartz (the principal) walks by—or we could just leave." I had no idea what to say.

Then Cindy said, "Well, I can't do this. I can't teach like this. I'm a science teacher. I can't teach a unit on freedom" (the topic we had been webbing in the in-service as an example). "There is absolutely no place for science in anything we were talking about down there. I can't teach like that."

And I lost it.

I felt all the frustration come up from the pit of my stomach, and I said something like, "Well Cindy I know how you feel . . . (and the tears started flowing). I feel so frustrated every day because that was the way I learned to teach. I wasn't trained to teach from a textbook. Everyday I feel so %@#! frustrated . . ." (I'm not sure if that was where I said %@)#!, but I said it) *"because I feel like I was hired to teach here because I do know how to teach like that, but nobody else in this place, or at least on this team, teaches like that or even wants to teach like that and I hate it!"*

At some point during this outburst, Elizabeth Milios walked in and said, "Well then, maybe you're in the wrong place! But don't you start blaming the team. It is not the team's fault. There are plenty of people in this school who would love to be on this team." Then Cindy pipes in with this: "Your insecurities and your inabilities are not my problem. You are not my problem. I don't care about your problems. I don't care about you!"

Ahh, yes, teaming at its finest.

At some point I told Elizabeth not to yell at me like I was one of her students, I did stop crying, but literally I felt like someone had dropped a barbell on my stomach. The rest of the day is a fog. We had to go down to the library to wrap things up. Everything in my whole being wanted to run away from that place. At the end of the in-service, one of the other new teachers, Reggie, looked at me and said, "Are you all right?" I looked at him and shook my head no, but I couldn't speak.

He said, "Come to my room." I followed him out of the library and the tears just started pouring out of my eyes. We got to his room and I started sobbing and I kept saying, "I can't do this. I can't do this. I thought I could but I can't. I have to resign. This is killing me. I can't do this."

Reggie just sat there on his knees and listened to me and he kept saying. "Don't quit. Don't quit. I'll help you. We'll do it together, whatever it takes. I swear I'll help you. You are meant to be a teacher."

What Will Happen? What Did Happen?

Three months after beginning what promised to be a stellar teaching career, Susan Jackson found herself crying on the floor of an eighth-grade public classroom, at a crossroads. Should she forge ahead or quit? Was the enthusiasm and energy, her love for teaching, knocked out of her so early in the game? What went wrong?

We share this story not to discourage current or future teachers but to generate thinking and to raise questions by all involved in the teaching profession. Was Susan's teacher preparation program inadequate? Were her goals too lofty? Were the teachers in Susan's school woefully uninformed or inflexible? Was Susan expecting too much? How typical is Susan experience?

We will return to Susan's story later, but before we do, we need to examine the foundation upon which Susan's teaching was built. Where did she get all those crazy ideas about active student involvement, about inquiry-based learning and problem solving, about student-designed curriculum, and about student-driven assessment? Where did these ideas come from? Are they new? Progressive? Or are these ideas old, maybe even very old?

Foundations of Constructivism: Forging a Way Back to the Future

2

This chapter looks at the origins of, and support for, Susan's ideas. We define constructivism, review the historical grounding and research that support constructivism, and examine the similarities between past and contemporary reform movements. One purpose of this chapter is to demonstrate that Susan had centuries of philosophical, theoretical, and practical backing for what she considered the real basics. (We will discuss other issues relating to Susan's experience throughout the book.) Another purpose is to provide the rationale for you to create a successful constructivist classroom and to encourage you to generate the powerful and critical questions that will lead you to positive, productive, and practical action.

What Exactly Is Constructivism?

It's About Constructing Knowledge, Not Receiving It

Constructivism is a theory about how we learn. If you were to write a definition or theory of learning, what would that be? What would be the core concepts? Would your definition be related to evaluation of a student's work? Would you describe learning in relation to a student's behavior or recitation? Would you relate it to your teaching? How would you—how do you—know when your students have learned? Would someone observing your classes be able to recognize learning as it occurred? Here is Aunt Addie's theory of learning:

> *I tell you one thing, if you learn it by yourself, if you have to get down and dig for it, it never leaves you. It stays here as long as you live because you had to dig it out of the mud before you learned it.* (Norton in Wigginton, 1986, Introduction)

The main proposition of constructivism is that learning means *constructing, creating, inventing,* and *developing* our own knowledge. Others can give us information, we can find information in books, and we can get information from the media, but as important as information is—and it is extremely important—receiving it, getting it, and hearing it does not necessarily equal learning. Learning in constructivist terms is:

- the process and the result of questioning, interpreting, and analyzing information;
- using this information and thinking process to develop, build, and alter our meaning and understanding of concepts and ideas; and
- integrating current experiences with our past experiences and what we already know about a given subject.

Each of us constructs our own meaning and learning about issues, problems, and topics. Because none of us has had exactly the same experiences as any other person, our understandings, our interpretations, and our schemata (knowledge constructs, learning) of any concept cannot be exactly the same as anyone else's. Our prior experiences, knowledge, and learning affect how we interpret and experience new events; our interpretations, in turn, affect construction of our knowledge structures and define our new learning.

Let's assume students are reading a story about a cat. Each student comes to class with a different understanding of the concept "cat." One student might be thinking cats are warm and cuddly; another might be thinking about how a cat's scratch can hurt. Given the meaning and past experiences each student has in relation to cats, the story itself takes on a different understanding for each student. Think about the day you were teaching about the causes of the Civil War or the seasons of the year, or any other subject. How many of your students really got it? How do you know how many understood in the way you meant it? Half of the students? Three quarters of the students? One student?

It is because we all make our own meanings and understandings of issues, concepts, and problems that the emphasis in a constructivist classroom is not on transmitting information but on promoting learning through student intellectual activity such as questioning, investigating, problem generating, and problem solving. It's about *constructing* knowledge, not receiving it.

It's About Thinking and Analyzing
(Crap Detecting), Not Accumulating and Memorizing

Frankly, I'm bored out of my gourd with it [classroom teaching]. . . . The essence of learning is the reading and research and application and what we've turned it into in the public schools is memory. (White in Page, 1992, p. 172)

Constructivism is about thinking and the thinking process rather than about the quantity of information a student can memorize and recite or, in the case of math for example, about answers based on memorized formulas. This does not mean that content is not important. On the contrary, content is very important; however, in a constructivist classroom, a teacher does not stand and deliver most or even much of the content material. Rather, students uncover, discover, and reflect on content and their conceptions of such through inquiry, investigation, research, and analysis in the context of a problem, critical question, issue, or theme. Students gain and are encouraged to develop through these processes the ability to think for themselves and to think critically; that is, to discriminate between the relevant and the irrelevant, to look at issues from different perspectives, to interpret and analyze written and electronic data, and, as some famous people—including George Plimpton (graduation speech, 1989), Postman and Weingartner (1969, p. 3), Ernest Hemingway (in Postman & Weingartner, p. 16), and songwriter Paul Simon in his song "Kodachrome" (1973)—would put it, to "detect crap."

It's About Understanding and Applying, Not Repeating Back

Constructivism focuses on in-depth understanding, not regurgitating and repeating back.

With the traditional education we're doing, people remember . . . 10% of what they learn. . . . They don't remember anything after the final exam anyway. . . . (White quoted in Page, 1992, p. 170)

Although some teachers call traditional education methods efficient in that they (the teachers) can transmit much material to students in a short amount of time, they do not consider how ineffective this delivery is in terms of students' understanding, retention, and application. How **do** you know if students understand concepts, issues, ideas, and problems? If a student repeats information, as often happens in a traditional class, it doesn't mean she understands anything or can apply this information in any way; it doesn't demonstrate learning or understanding—it simply demonstrates the ability to repeat information. In a constructivist classroom, students demonstrate their learning and understanding through various means. They might develop new critical questions; they might write a script for a video; they might summarize key ideas in their own words; they might produce or create something; and/or they might frame and solve problems.

It's About Being Active, Not Passive

There is no such thing as genuine knowledge and fruitful understanding except as offspring of doing. (Dewey, 1916, p. 321)

Although information is important, passively accumulating disconnected information is not learning. Passively receiving ready-made knowledge from someone or something else is not learning. To learn, a student has to be mentally and often physically active. A student learns (that is, builds knowledge structures) when she discovers her own answers, solutions, concepts, and relationships and creates her own interpretations. Although constructivists differ on details of the concept of learning, all propose that when students conduct their own learning, discover their own answers, and create their own interpretations, their learning is deeper, more comprehensive, and longer lasting; and the learning that occurs actively leads to an ability to think critically (Dewey, 1933; Freire, 1981; Kilpatrick, 1918, 1929; Sharan & Sharan, 1989/1990; Wigginton, 1989). They also all agree that learning is not what Goodlad (1984) described in his study of schooling. Learning is **not**

. . . a lot of teacher talk and a lot of student listening; almost invariably closed and factual questions; little corrective feedback and not guidance; and predominantly total class instructional configuration around traditional activities—all in a virtually affectless environment. (p. 242)

It also is not what a high school student described:

I don't do a lot in school. . . . I don't like any of the high school classes really. You just sit there and they tell you something and they give you a test and you tell it right back to them. Everybody has the same answer on the test if you do it right. (Clark in Page, 1992, Introduction)

Historical Roots: What's New Is Really Old: Or, Looking Back to the Future

Traditional Education Versus Constructivism

Traditional education is "guaranteed to **rot** your brain" (Commager, 1980, p. 34). One of the themes that all proponents of constructivism (active learning) have in common is the rejection of the traditional teacher-dominated classroom in which the teacher manages, controls, and dispenses the information (Page, 1990). They see this education not only as passive and controlling but also dysfunctional in relation to individual, democratic, and societal needs. They see it as stifling students' creativity, autonomy, independent thinking, competence, confidence, and self-esteem and as making students dependent, conforming, and nonthinking.

On the other hand, active learning is guaranteed to **expand** the brain. Let's take a look at how some well-known educators, philosophers, and psychologists felt and feel about traditional education and what they thought and think about more powerful ways to engage students in learning. The historical connections and progressions allow us to make sense of constructivism today and to understand where Susan got some of her ideas.

Rousseau and Pestalozzi

Jean-Jacques Rousseau (1762/1957) lived during the age known as the Enlightenment and is thought by many to have inspired the French Revolution with his stinging essays on society and government. He believed that the classical education of his time, which consisted of reading and memorizing, prevented students from being active, which in turn caused them to be passive, destructive, deceitful, selfish, and stupid. He argued that this education was boring and beyond the child's comprehension, and that it taught students "to believe much and know little" (p. 90).

Rousseau's *Emile* (1762/1957), his treatise on what education should be, is often considered the foundation of progressivism (Sahakian & Sahakian, 1974) or of what today we would call constructivism. Rousseau (1762/1957) believed that students learn through their senses, experience, and activity. Through the senses, the child discovers, compares, and judges what he experiences, and what results are impressions called ideas. Reasoning, Rousseau asserted, is the act of sorting, associating, connecting, and discriminating among and between these simple ideas to form complex ideas and relationships. It is the child's interaction with the environment—his experiences—that correct and modify these ideas and that results in true learning. For Rousseau, the core concept of learning would be a compound of ideas.

Johann Heinrich Pestalozzi (1801/1898), a disciple of Rousseau, devoted much of his life to teaching the orphans of the French Revolution. Like Rousseau, Pestalozzi claimed that classical education that was "blown in their ears" (p. 244), made students anxious, confused, and passive. He noted that students memorized information but did not understand. Instead, Pestalozzi (1801/1898) argued that the student's mind receives impressions through observation and experience and that these impressions produce ideas and an organized mental structure that enables the student to compare, examine, separate, sort, and conclude. He used the term *anschauung* (p.7) to refer to the mental process through which the ideas and mental structures are developed. He claimed this process by which people formed concepts and ideas was the source of all human cognition.

Dewey and Kilpatrick

When John Dewey opened his laboratory school in Chicago in 1896, American education was essentially the classical education of Pestalozzi's time and similar to the education Dewey himself had experienced as boring (Campbell, 1971). Dewey objected to the content and method of this classical education because it did not involve problem solving or reflective thinking. Instead, students memorized and recited unrelated chunks of material (Dewey, 1931/1970) and became docile (Dewey, 1938/1972).

For Dewey, the central idea was intellectual integration. He described (1931/1970) the mind in a mentally active student as "roaming far and wide" but returning with what it found and constantly making judgments as to relationships, relevancies, and bearings on a central theme. This process of integration included seeking, finding, using, organizing, digesting, and assimilating information. Like Rousseau and Pestalozzi before him, Dewey (1933, 1938/1972) talked about the interaction between the learner and the environment. His theory was that what one learned in one situation helped to direct the understanding and action of future situations. This person or environment interaction led to a continual reconstruction of impulses and thought. Dewey described the mind as a verb, as something to do rather than something to be filled like a sponge. He believed that because students need to interact with their environment in order to think, every student should be engaged in activity around a project (Dewey, 1933; Ernst, 1953). For projects to be educative, Dewey (1933) argued, they needed to fit the student's interest, involve the student actively, have intrinsic worth, present problems that would lead to new questions and inquiry, and involve a considerable time span.

William Heard Kilpatrick, a graduate student of Dewey, claimed that the inflexibility of traditional classroom setups and of the traditional teacher-student relationship squelched natural ability and led to passive and unintelligent conformity (Connell, 1980; Kilpatrick, 1929). He argued that teachers were concerned mainly with students being able to recite material without error (Tyler, 1975). He asserted that thinking is the intelligent, interactive adaptation between the person and the environment

(Kilpatrick, 1933/1969). Although Kilpatrick's idea of project work involved more student autonomy than did Dewey's, Kilpatrick, like Dewey, believed that projects should be the center of the curriculum because they would increase student motivation and involvement, turn boring schoolwork into meaningful activity, and at the same time increase student knowledge and skill.

Piaget and Bruner

Jean Piaget, a Swiss biologist and psychologist interested in how humans adapted to the environment, met several times with American educators—including John Dewey—during the 1920s and 1930s. He expanded on Dewey's argument against traditional education with his claim that the traditional instructional method of *teacher telling* students required that the teacher and the student (listener) have mutual communication frameworks but that this was not realistic. He argued that a student heard what he perceived which might not be the same thing as what the teacher was saying. What teachers taught, therefore, was not always what the students learned (Labinowicz, 1980; Piaget, 1941/1995).

One cannot overestimate Piaget's contributions to the direction, meaning, and understanding of contemporary constructivism. Here we present two of his most important ideas about how people learn. First, Piaget gives us the term *schemata*, which refers to knowledge structures or constructs and ways of perceiving, understanding, and thinking about the world. According to Piaget, learners construct their own knowledge schemes in relation to, and filtered through, previous and current experiences. Second, Piaget described mental development (learning) as a process of equilibrium in response to external stimuli. That is, in the interaction with the environment, he theorized, the student assimilates complementary components of the external world into his existing cognitive structures (schemata); if new experiences do not fit the existing knowledge structures or schemes, the student will change or alter those structures to accommodate the new information. The processes of assimilation and accommodation create equilibrium (Piaget, 1967/1971; Weil & Murphy, 1982). When an external disturbance causes disequilibrium, he believed, the student has to think in order to resolve the conflict. The process of maintaining equilibrium—construction and reconstruction of knowledge—in relation to the environment is what creates cognitive growth (Piaget, 1967/1971; Labinowicz, 1980). Therefore, in Piaget's view, for knowledge to be truly meaningful, students need to construct it themselves.

Jerome Bruner, a psychologist, met and worked with Piaget and also was one of the group of American scholars, educators, and scientists who, during the late 1950s and early 1960s, were rewriting math, science, and social studies curricula as a result of the educational debate that occurred after the launching of Sputnik. (They called it the "new science," the "new math," and the "new social studies.") Like those already mentioned, Bruner rejects the teacher-as-knowledge-dispenser model of traditional education (Bruner, 1961). He claims, as did Dewey and Kilpatrick, that the teaching of information out of context results in rote nonsense because the delivered content is not connected to or associated with student action, and students do not form the necessary cognitive connections to understand the material (Bruner, 1971).

Discovery is the core of Bruner's theory. Whatever a person discovers for himself is what he truly knows. From discovery, Bruner asserts, comes increased intellectual ability, including the ability to solve problems. This discovery is a matter of students thinking about and rearranging material in terms of their interests and cognitive structures (Bruner's phrase for schemata) in a way that leads to new insights and new inquiry. The goal is for students to be autonomous and self-propelled thinkers (Bruner, 1961).

Freire, Wigginton, and Sharan

Paulo Freire, a South American scholar and revolutionary, described traditional education as involving a vertical relationship in which teachers are on top, students are on the bottom, and there is no room for student dialogue. He saw traditional education as working *on* a student rather than *with* him. As did Rousseau, Pestalozzi, Dewey, and Kilpatrick before him, Freire (1981) asserted that this traditional education forces students to conform to the existing social system (Freire, 1974). Freire (1974) called this the banking model of education. In this model, which he rejected, the teacher (the banker) makes deposits into the passive accounts (the students). They receive and file the deposits, and that is that.

For Freire, education should involve a critical dialogue and an active search for knowledge that leads to positive action in society. Students need to question, to create and re-create, and to participate actively in their own learning. When interacting with the environment, Freire (1981) asserted, the student discovers and mentally organizes knowledge. This knowledge or learning becomes the basis for knowledge that will replace it. Freire, like Dewey, believed that gaining knowledge requires constant searching and that the only person who learns is the one who invents and reinvents his learning and then uses it in concrete situations. He called this mentally organized knowledge.

Elliot Wigginton was a high school teacher for over 25 years in Georgia. He describes students in traditional classrooms as bored receivers, who are glued to lectures, burdened by unreadable text books, and forced to memorize information irrelevant to their lives. In that traditional classroom, the teacher is the boss and has all the knowledge. The result is rebellious and alienated students. Wigginton's (1986) epiphany for the need for active learning was at least in part a result of students setting on fire the podium from which he was lecturing. (What was it Rousseau said about students becoming destructive?)

In response, Wigginton created the Foxfire program that began as a way for students to learn English/language arts by collecting and documenting oral histories of people in their own communities. Wigginton believes—similarly to Rousseau, Pestalozzi, Dewey, and Kilpatrick—that what the student learns and figures out for himself is what he knows. Actions leading to discoveries are internalized (cognitive processes) and remembered; and projects, he believes, should flow from the student's own interests, reflections, and evaluations. Problem solving, as advocated by Dewey, should not be an end in itself but should lead to other questions and problems.

Not as well known, but with a similar message, is Shlomo Sharan, professor emeritus at Tel Aviv University and developer of the cooperative learning program called

Group Investigation. Like Bruner, Sharan (Sharan, 1985; Sharan & Sharan, 1992) claims that the traditional teaching model, in which the teacher dominates and transmits knowledge and the student is passive, does not allow the student to process information and therefore does not lead to any meaning or comprehension for the student.

Sharan (Sharan, 1985; Sharan & Sharan, 1992) believes that students learn best through problem solving. Topics and methods of learning become personally relevant to the students when they engage in the process of investigation typical of a particular discipline or profession—that is, in a science class, the students work as scientists; in a history class, students work as historians. Like Dewey and Piaget, Sharan believes that through active learning the student organizes and assimilates the experience and that this process helps the student to develop logical thought and higher-order thinking skills. He believes that students understand events in relation to their past experiences and level of development.

Although not all the individuals we discuss above would necessarily have used or would use the word "constructivist" to describe themselves, the core concept of their theories of learning revolve around the same propositions:

- Students learn more when they are actively engaged in their own learning.
- By investigating and discovering for themselves, by creating and re-creating, and by interacting with the environment, students build their own knowledge structures and the ability to think critically and to solve problems.
- Learning actively leads to an ability to think critically and to solve problems.
- Through an active learning approach, students learn content and process at the same time (Page, 1990).

The core concept of their theories of learning was and is that students construct their own knowledge when they are mentally active in or on their environment.

QUESTION:

? *Why are these philosophers, psychologists, and educators all men? Where are all the great women thinkers? What women in history, and contemporary times, warrant a place here and why?*

Coming of Age: Active Learning
Movements From the Early 1900s to Today

The Activity Movement, which was part of the Progressive Education Movement of the early 1900s, evolved from Kilpatrick's project method. The premise of this movement was that acquiring and developing knowledge should be an active (mental and physical) process that should involve a project. Keep in mind that this did not mean students could or should do whatever they felt like or wanted to do. The movement stressed that:

- there should be enough different kinds of projects to allow all students to succeed;
- the work should be cooperative;
- the interests and needs of the student should determine the nature of the project; and
- school organization should be democratic.

The Activity Movement became so large that in 1934 the National Society for the Study of Education devoted an entire volume of its *33rd Yearbook* to its study. The study reported the following positive aspects of the activity method:

- It improves students' abilities to think, plan, and do.
- It develops initiative.
- It leads to better understanding of life.
- It creates new student/teacher relationships.
- It provides motivation.
- It increases the students' interest in school.
- It leads students to read more.
- It allows for more self-expression.
- It leads to standards of achievement in subject areas as high as or higher than in a traditional method.

The Progressive educators and philosophers and the activity movements of the early 1900s provided the foundations for the contemporary active learning movements. The 1980s and 1990s gave birth to, or saw reinvented or revived from past eras, constructivist-based, active learning movements based on the work of the important thinkers we discuss above. These recent movements include the elementary school Whole Language movement (MacInnis & Hemming, 1995), middle school reforms (Carnegie, 1989; 2000), and high school restructuring (National Association of Secondary School Principals [NASSP], 1996; Sizer, 1996). The first edition of *Creating and Sustaining the Constructivist Classroom* looks at these movements in detail (Marlowe & Page, 1998).

But since the publication of our first edition, and with the onslaught of the standardized testing requirements, these and similar reform movements appear to have become covert. For fear of retaliation—through withholding of funding, threat of job loss, and other insidious processes—these movements have become hidden somewhat, at least in the literature if not in reality. Why then should teachers bother? Why? Because the research supporting constructivist classrooms is simply impossible to ignore; it's just too overwhelming. In the next chapter, we look at the empirical research results that support the *why* of constructivist approaches, and additionally, we review what the professional teacher organizations have to say about teaching and learning.

What Do the Experts Say? Listening to the Research and Professional Teachers' Organizations

3

Research Results

Past and contemporary research results on the use of active learning methods associated with the tenets of constructivism are impressive and consistently positive. The greatest difference between the older research and the newest research is in the sophistication of the contemporary research tools and methods. The research as a whole shows active learning methods to be superior to teacher-dominated teaching approaches in measures of academic, affective, and skill learning. Here we review only a few of the most important findings. For a detailed appraisal of the remarkable scope and power of the vast body of research that supports constructivist practices see Alfie Kohn's (2000) *The Schools our Children Deserve*.

Looking Back (The First Half of the 20th Century)

Two of the most groundbreaking studies demonstrating the power of constructivist approaches occurred before World War II. In the first, in a study of the project method, research demonstrated that Winnetka Elementary School students (Washburne & Raths, 1927), who worked on projects during the first half of the day and on individualized subject matter during the second half, were better prepared than those students from three traditional classrooms in other towns of similar social composition. Perhaps most dramatically, the Winnetka students, who joined the students of the three other towns in a regional high school, were the only ones who scored above average on all major subject tests.

The most extensive early research study of active learning methods and results began in 1933. The Progressive Education Association (Aiken, 1942) conducted the now famous Eight Year Study, which involved 30 high schools implementing progressive innovations. All the schools used activities and methods based on the principles of active learning discussed above and so clearly described since the time of Rousseau and for centuries before. Three hundred colleges agreed to eliminate standard entrance requirements for graduates of these high schools and to accept the students on the basis of their interest and their ability to work successfully as determined by the high school

(Greene, 1942). The researchers matched 1,475 of the original 2,000 progressive students with graduates of conventional schools in terms of scholastic aptitude, interests, and socioeconomic background. The first follow-up began in 1936 as the first graduates entered college. Researchers added a new graduating class each year until 1939. Based on these students' college records, instructors' reports, written work, and student questionnaires and interviews, the authors concluded that graduates of the progressive schools were "on the whole" (Aiken, 1942, p. 149) more successful than their matches and that students whose high school programs were most different from traditional programs were much superior to their traditional school counterparts (Aiken, 1942; Darling-Hammond, 1993; Greene, 1942; Walten & Travers, 1963).

What's Happened More Recently?

Since the 1960s, every decade has produced major research support for constructivist propositions about learning. Here we take a look at a few of the highlights.

1960s

- A six-week study by Worthen (1968) involved 423 fifth- and sixth-grade math students, half learning with a discovery method and the other half being taught by direct teacher instruction. This study showed the teacher-dominated method to be superior on initial recall but the discovery method to be superior on retention and transfer.

- For several studies (Massialas & Zevin, 1967) involving different social studies classes in two Chicago high schools over a three-year period, teachers developed and used new discovery materials and approaches. Analysis of interview data showed that with discovery approaches:
    - there was a greater exchange of ideas between students;
    - student participation doubled;
    - students learned how to organize and form hypotheses and to use, interpret, and apply evidence; and
    - students looked at knowledge as tentative rather than absolute.

1970s

- In a comparative study of two learning methods, Phillips and Faris (1977) concluded that students probably will learn more if given the chance to do so in nontraditional ways. In their study of two groups of senior government students, one group worked in the traditional lecture and discussion mode; the other group used innovative and active learning techniques including independent study and internships. The active learning students surpassed the traditional students in achievement after the first few weeks.

1980s

- The Sudbury Valley School in Framingham, Massachusetts, is a K–12 school with no entrance or learning requirements. The school supports student-directed activities and offers courses only when students show interest. There are no grades and no evaluations. To graduate, the student has to defend a thesis at a meeting of the school's Assembly and has to prove he is ready to take responsibility for himself. Gray and Chanoff (1986) conducted a follow-up study of 78 graduates. At the time these graduates had entered the Sudbury School, more than one-third of them had had serious school problems including truancy, rebellion, learning disabilities, anxiety, and emotional disturbances. The authors surveyed the graduates using questionnaires, telephone contact, and personal interviews. The data revealed that there were no apparent difficulties being admitted to college and that the graduates were successful in a wide range of careers. Students reported that the school had helped them develop their own interests and responsibility as well as to develop initiative, curiosity, the ability to communicate with all people, and an appreciation of democratic values.

- A study of Group Investigation, a cooperative learning approach focusing on higher-level learning (Sharan & Shachar 1988), involved eighth-grade classes in Israel. Four classes used traditional teaching methods and four used the Group Investigation method. Teachers were assigned at random and participated in a series of training workshops during the pilot part of the study. During the actual experiment, there were 197 students in the Group Investigation and 154 in the traditional group. Results based on pre- and post-tests, student-prepared discussions, and videotapes showed a highly superior level of achievement in the Group Investigation classes as compared to the traditional classes in both higher- and lower-level thinking.

- Finally, as the focus on active learning heightened, Bredderman (1983) conducted a meta-review of the effectiveness of process-oriented science programs involving 57 studies. He found significant gains in creativity, intelligence, language use, and math.

1990s

- A study (Page, 1992) of the National History Day Program, a grade 6–12 program grounded in active learning propositions, showed that the participating students developed their own conclusions and their own knowledge. Additionally, the students expressed a deeper awareness of issues involved in the topics they were researching and believed that they had learned content better, had higher comprehension, and had obtained transferable skills to a greater degree than was possible in a traditional classroom.

- In 1993, researchers from Vanderbilt University; the University of California, Berkeley; and the Ontario Institute for Studies in Education developed a project called Schools for Thought. The underlying foundation for this project is the belief that students construct their own knowledge. Classrooms in the Schools for Thought program focus on students developing *critical thinking skills*, such as acquiring and analyzing information through inquiry and investigation, and on student communication of findings to authentic adult audiences. The main principles of the program include:

1. student choice of research topics within a teacher-determined and core content framework;

2. group work;

3. individual student accountability;

4. integration of process and content;

5. creation of authentic products and involvement of authentic audiences such as community members; and

6. authentic use of technology.

In comparing student achievement in a sixth-grade Schools for Thought program in Nashville to student achievement in other classrooms, researchers found that on "10 subtests of the TCAP [Tennessee Comprehensive Assessment Program] . . . students scored as well as, or significantly better than, the comparison classes on all of the subtests" (Secules, Cottom, Bray, & Miller, 1997, p. 58). On a complex performance assessment that measured high-level critical thinking skills, Schools for Thought students scored significantly higher than students in other classrooms (Secules et al., 1997).

2000s

• Fraser and Spinner (2002) compared fifth-grade students in two constructivist math classes with fifth-grade students in four traditional math classes. Pre- and post-testing—including conceptual map testing (Novak in Fraser & Spinner, 2002) and the Test of Mathematics-Related Attitudes—indicated that the constructivist Class Banking System (CBS) program students had dramatic results in their (1) understanding of math concepts, (2) attitudes toward mathematics, and (3) perceptions of the classroom environment. Data also showed that higher cognitive achievement was found consistently in the experimental groups as compared to the control groups. Additional interviewing and observation of two control sets and one experimental set of students supported these findings. CBS is an interdisciplinary, individualized curriculum and process in which students solve personal and community issues through math application.

The research base is clear and growing. Active learning programs in which students construct and apply their own knowledge lead to the development of critical and independent thinking skills, deeper understanding of concepts and longer-lasting learning. We can't ignore these findings. Dewey's ideas are alive and well in our own post-industrial times. One thing is new, advocates argue: Ideas that in the past were supported merely by the armchair theorizing of influential philosophers today are grounded in empirical evidence (Donmoyer, 1996).

Although this research provides support for anyone wanting to implement constructivist activities in his or her classroom, in the long run, what matters are *your* findings, *your* results, *your* observations, and *your* experiences. If you and your students can develop successful active learning programs and experience positive results connected to your efforts, that is the real test.

From Coming of Age to Being an Endangered Species

In spite of the avalanche of anecdotal and empirical reports concerning the positive results of progressive, active learning and in spite of mounds of literature chronicling the need for reform in the schools, the entrenched and passive traditional practices persist. From the 1960s to the 2000s (the same time frame during which we see the developing body of supportive research), we see a substantial lack of progress in developing constructivist classrooms.

In 1978, the National Science Foundation released a seven-volume report on the status of math, science, and social studies education (Puckett, 1986). This report found that the "dominant mode of instruction to be large group, teacher-controlled recitation and lecture, based primarily on the textbook" (Shaver, Davis, & Helburn in Puckett, 1986, p. 390). Those results are basically the same as the results from three studies in the 1980s by Goodlad (1984), Boyer (1983), and Sizer (1984) that concluded that "classroom practice is largely devoid of student inquiry, discovery learning, and other innovative strategies" (Puckett, 1986, p. 389).

When Cuban (1983) examined changes since 1870 in theory, curriculum, and resources in relation to classroom instruction, he found that although theories, philosophies, textbooks, and curricula had changed, there was little evidence of change in teacher practice and that teacher dominated instruction was remarkably stable at all levels of schooling even though reformers have and had been fighting against teacher-dominated instruction since the mid-1850s (Cuban, 1983, 1990). Cuban found similar entrenched practices in his most recent research (Cuban, 2001, 2004; Cuban, Kirkpatrick & Peck, 2001).

Taking the Bull by the Horns: Why Is the Time Now?

We can go back to Rousseau, to the ancient Greeks, or even to prehistoric man to find a rationale for active learning approaches, but if Cuban (1990, 2004) found little change in teacher-dominated methods in the last 100 years, what might make it happen now? Two things: First, our need for such approaches is more urgent now than ever. A teacher-dominated instructional system that delivers information cannot work in an age of information explosion. Estimates 20 years ago (Hartoonian, 1984) were that information would henceforth increase 100% every 24 months. A more recent estimate (School of Information Management and Systems [SIMS], 2003) is that information doubled from 2000 to 2003 and will continue to double every three years. Whether it is doubling every two years or every three years, exponentially the growth each year is huge. There is no way teachers and students can manage that amount of information in a traditional "teacher-telling," "student-listening" approach. Second, the student who passively receives information has no notion of what it means to be a responsible citizen in a democratic society (Page, 2002) or to be a worker who must take initiative and responsibility. Our democracy relies on citizens who can find, understand, and use information to make productive decisions for themselves and their country; as is, our education system is failing to prepare citizens for this responsibility.

Professional Teachers' Organizations

Although practice may not reflect what research says ought to be happening, surprisingly we find the active learning propositions of constructivism alive and well in the current discipline-area learning and teacher performance standards frameworks. There have been changes in some of the national learning standards in the last few years. This is most notable in the math and science standards in terms of greater emphasis on content items. The pressure of the standardized testing movement led to these changes. However, what is important is that all of the standards frameworks still have at their heart the values, propositions, and beliefs in the power and necessity of active learning processes, and these frameworks emphasize the learning rather than the teaching process.

NCTE: National Council of Teachers of English/Language Arts

In 1993, the National Council of Teachers of English (NCTE) reported that the methods for teaching literature in secondary schools still remained quite traditional. They described this approach as teacher dominated and revolving around whole-class discussions that were meant to direct students to one common understanding. The *Standards for the English Language Arts* (1996), developed by the NCTE and the International Reading Association, proposed to change this traditional approach to a learner-centered focus. The standards advocate problem solving and application in real situations.

MOST RECENT ENGLISH/LANGUAGE ARTS FRAMEWORK:

There are no more recent NCTE learning standards than the 1996 edition. However, the recent (2003) pilot edition of the National College Association of Teacher Education (NCATE) standards for teachers of English and the Language Arts (www.ncate.org/standard/programstds.htm, 2003) continues the focus on the need for teachers to engage students in critical thinking, critical analysis, and research. Additionally the standards require teachers to use a wide range of approaches to (1) allow students to draw on their past experiences and backgrounds in analyzing and understanding materials and (2) to assist students in constructing meanings from all forms of media.

These standards are consistent with and supportive of a constructivist approach to teaching and learning.

NCTM: National Council of Teachers of Mathematics

As with other national standards, those from the National Council of Teachers of Mathematics (NCTM) argue that current traditional practices have to change and that we can no longer accept that our students need problem solving "only on Wednesdays," as reported by one of our graduate students in his survey of local teacher practice. The focus of the 1992 *Curriculum and Evaluation Standards for School Mathematics* (NCTM, 1992) was on active learning; these standards stressed that students need to discover why formulas and procedures work rather than how to follow them; to understand rather than memorize; to create and solve math problems related to real life; and to move from thinking that there is one right answer to focusing on mathematical reasoning. The companion booklet, *Assessment Standards for School Mathematics* (NCTM, 1995), reiterated that there must be a shift in emphasis from students listening and memorizing to student inquiry and investigation. This document blames traditional methods for perpetuating the myth that some students simply can't do math. It clearly defines the teacher's role as questioning, listening, and setting high expectations, and it describes assessment as a way to determine students' understanding as a stepping-stone to future learning.

MOST RECENT MATH FRAMEWORK:

The newest math learning standards (NCTM, 2000) as well as the most recent NCATE teacher performance standards for math teachers (www.ncate.org/standard/ programstds.htm, 2003) focus on the same principles as those in the 1992 and 1995 documents. The focus is on conceptual understanding rather than memorization, building new knowledge from experience and prior knowledge, and on students having control of their learning. Additionally, the standards support the need for students to be able to analyze and solve problems, formulate questions and analyze data, reason statistically, and to connect math concepts to daily lives and to other disciplines—all consistent with constructivist theories and approaches.

NSTA: National Science Teachers Association

The themes in the science standards can be framed in a single phrase: *Science as inquiry*. As with studies reported by the NCTE, findings from a 1993 survey of science and math education showed that although hands-on activities had increased in science classes, the largest proportion of class time in science was still being spent listening to lecture (Association for Supervision and Curriculum Development [ASCD], 1995). The 1996 science content standards developed by the National Science Teachers Association and the National Research Council encourage students to make meaning for themselves through active investigation; the *National Science Education Standards* also focus on learning science as an active process and on student understanding and on the use of investigative and problem-solving processes (National Research Council, 1996).

MOST RECENT SCIENCE FRAMEWORK:

The 2003 Standards of Science Teachers (National Research Council, 2003) is based on a review of the 1996 Science Standards and supports and amplifies the need to prepare scientifically literate citizens who can use scientific approaches for analyzing and solving problems.

Additionally, the 2003 Teacher Standards stipulate that teachers need to be able to engage students in active learning through scientific inquiry, encourage students to observe, question, design inquiry, and collect and interpret data in order to reach conclusions. The Standards recommend a variety of active learning approaches including concept mapping, role-playing, simulation, questioning, and developing projects—once again, consistent with and supportive of constructivist propositions.

NCSS: The National Council of Social Studies

There are two sets of standards in the social studies world. The first set is from the world of History. The 1994 National History Standards (National Center for History in the Schools, 1994) and the revised standards (1996) focus on students finding and interpreting records and constructing solid historical arguments and conclusions. The second set of standards is from the National Council of Social Studies. *Charting a Course: Social Studies for the 21st Century,* the report of the National Commission on Social Studies in the Schools (1989), not only proposed active learning (researching, organizing, and analyzing and interpreting data) but also went so far as to suggest that students should develop their own curricular materials (Page, 1992).

MOST RECENT SOCIAL STUDIES FRAMEWORK:
NOT RECENT AT ALL AND FALLING BEHIND:

The 1994 contribution from the National Council of Social Studies, Expectations of Excellence: Curriculum Standards for Social Studies, focuses on the preparation of an active, participatory citizenry. This means that students need to be able to analyze and interpret all forms of media, look at issues from different perspectives, and to compare different positions in order to make informed reasoned decisions for the public good. The National Standards for Social Studies Teachers (NCSS, 1997) support the need for and recommend learner-centered, active instruction. However, these frameworks are now 10 and 7 years old. The National History Standards are also 10 years old. The lack of current frameworks could have something to do with the fact that there are no standardized tests at this point for the social studies.

Teachers of social studies would do themselves a favor to become familiar with the political schism between the NCSS organization and organizations more focused on the study of history. It appears that the time is ripe to have input into up-to-date frameworks.

Although the newest of the standards publications, especially in math and science, show a definite move to a greater focus on specific content, all of the disciplines and their respective organizations at their core continue to have constructivist propositions of student inquiry, problem solving, decision making, and understanding rather than teacher-directed programs of memorization and recitation.

Checking Your Understanding: What Exactly Is Constructivism?

Changing your classroom from a traditional one to a constructivist one will not happen overnight. It is a progressive process that requires doing and reflecting, more doing and reflecting, and then more doing and reflecting. You may, in fact, have first experiences similar to Susan's. The key to successful efforts, in addition to your ongoing reflection and persistence, is in your clear understanding of the constructivist concepts and what those concepts look like when applied in a classroom.

Following is a list of statements made either by students in our Learning Theory classes or by teachers with whom we have worked who are involved in making changes in their classrooms. Let's take a look at where your current understanding of constructivism is. Remember: *Constructivism is a theory about how people learn.* It is a theory that says that learning means constructing and developing one's own knowledge; that we do this by actively questioning, interpreting, problem solving, and creating; and that in-depth understanding is one result of this learning. Take the challenge. Mark off the statements with which you agree.

CHALLENGE STATEMENTS

	A field trip is a constructivist activity.
	Constructivist classes do not have quizzes.
	If students are sitting in rows, then it's not a constructivist class.
	Science lab experiments are examples of constructivism.
	In a constructivist class, students have fun.
	These students are involved in a geography project; it must be a constructivist class.
	The students could choose their own topics; therefore, it must be a constructivist assignment.
	If a student can give a presentation, then it means that he/she must understand the material.
	Developing a presentation using PowerPoint is a constructivist activity.
	This class was a constructivist's dream—the students were moving around and communicating with one another.

(Continued)

CHALLENGE STATEMENTS (Continued)

	This is a constructivist class. You know that because the students are working in groups.
	Cooperative learning is an excellent example of a constructivist activity.
	The students in this class are focusing on state learning standards. This cannot be a constructivist classroom.
	If the teacher is preparing students for standardized testing, this cannot be a constructivist classroom.

With how many statements did you agree? Which ones were they? Remember again that constructivism is a theory about how people learn. Review the statements using this as a frame of reference. Do you still agree with the same statements? Give yourself one point for each statement with which you agreed.

Scoring Guide

- If you scored between 9 and 14, don't waste another minute; read and study the rest of this book as quickly as possible.
- If you scored between 4 and 8, categorize the statements with which you agreed by issues and look at the chapters that address these issues.
- If you scored 3 or less, and it is because you feel there isn't enough information in any of the statements to clarify and define learning, *please* don't leave education. Students need you.

Why does a high score suggest the need for more study of the tenets of constructivism? The answer is that there is not enough information in any of these statements to allow you to determine whether the statement is valid. For example, if the field trip is teacher directed and students are simply filling in blanks on a worksheet without investigating, discovering, and problem solving, it would not be constructivist. Likewise, just because students are working in groups, it does not mean they are involved in a constructivist activity. We would have to know more about the purpose and context of the activity and also about the kind of student-to-student communication and interaction that was or was not occurring in the groups. Similarly, whether or not students are focusing on state learning standards does not tell us what kind of learning approach is involved.

We suggest that you revisit the statements above often as you work your way through the book and as you become more familiar with what constructivism looks like in a classroom.

The Road Map

The problem now is the same as it has been in the past. There are few guidelines to help teachers make the transition from the traditional approach to teaching and learning to an active approach. How will creating a constructivist classroom affect you and your students? Ultimately, if you take your time and reflect and act appropriately on results, student learning and your place and role in the classroom can change drastically for the better. There is no one way to create a constructivist classroom, and, as you know from Susan's story, there are no guarantees. Constructivist classrooms don't all look or work the same way. Like life, this is more of a journey than a destination. If you are ready to start the journey, it's time to do some self-diagnostic work. Consider the following tough questions and then read on.

TOUGH QUESTIONS:

1. *At what point would a more teacher-directed approach make more sense than a constructivist approach? Why?*

2. *How can a teacher balance a student's need for discovery, exploration, and invention with the student's need for structure?*

3. *Susan Jackson understood the constructivist ideas advocated in the middle school reform efforts. Her knowledge base included much about appropriate middle school organization, the needs of young adolescents, interdisciplinary teaming, constructivist learning theory, and student-developed curriculum. Based on her letter (Chapter 1) written at the beginning of her teaching experience in a middle school, in what way(s) had her teacher preparation program failed her?*

4. *It appears that reform efforts are the slowest at the high school level. Why do you think this might be so?*

5. *If all the professional teachers' organizations have developed standards grounded in constructivist propositions, why haven't classrooms made drastic changes to meet these standards? How would you go about creating a plan in your school to address the standards?*

6. *Is standards-based instruction incompatible with constructivism? Why? Why not?*

Self Assessment: Look Before, While, and After You Leap

Before you can create a constructivist class, you will need to assess where you are in practice and philosophy, so we begin with the concept and process of self-assessment for the teacher. In this chapter, we will examine: (1) how what you say, even to yourself, affects the way your students and you approach teaching and learning; (2) the importance of classroom communication; (3) teacher and student roles; (4) classroom management; and (5) motivation.

Assessing Your Language

If you have tried already to make the shift from a traditional classroom to an active learning environment and have not had expected results, or if you want to try to make some changes now, first you will need to look at subtle and not-so-subtle dynamics in your classroom. We will start by asking you to complete Checklist 4.1. Indicate how often each statement is true in this checklist and in all the other checklists throughout this chapter. Add all total scores, and then go to the last page of the chapter to find out what your score means.

✔ CHECKLIST 4.1	4	3	2	1
	Always	Almost Always	Sometimes	Never
I use the words "discover" or "uncover" instead of "cover."				
I use the words "investigation" or "exploration" instead of "unit."				
I use the word "learn" instead of "teach."				
I use the phrase "learning experience" instead of "presentation."				
I use the phrase "student learning plan" instead of "lesson plan."				
			TOTAL SCORE	

Once you complete Checklist 4.1, the challenge is to review the five words or phrases that are key to making changes in your classroom. Table 4.1 is only half complete. The side that is complete represents the language perhaps you and students use and hear in a traditional classroom. We would recommend some kind of penance if we thought it would help you to eliminate it. What it will take is tremendous concentration and discipline on your part to make some changes here. Fill in the constructivist half of the table with language you think will lead to a different focus and a more student-engaged and student-powered dynamic.

TABLE 4.1

Traditional	Constructivist
1. Today I will be **teaching** about the about the Civil War.	
2. I always have to change my **lesson plans.**	
3. I have to **cover** fractions this week.	
4. What **unit** are you working on?	
5. How many of you have your **presentations** ready?	

See Table 4.2 to see the changes we would recommend.

TABLE 4.2

Traditional	Constructivist
1. Today I will be **teaching** about the Civil War.	Today you (the students) will be **learning** about the Civil War.
2. I always have to change my **lesson plans.**	You have to modify your **learning plans.**
3. I have to **cover** fractions this week.	Next week you will **discover** how fractions work.
4. What **unit** are you working on?	What are you **investigating?**
5. How many of you have your **presentations** ready?	How many of you have your **interactive learning experiences** (ILEs) ready?

Why These Changes?

The language that most teachers use is the language they know; that is, the language they experienced themselves as students. That language has its origin in the traditional, behaviorist system that more often than not defines learning as acquiring, accumulating, and memorizing information. Traditional language not only does not work in a constructivist classroom but also hinders creation and sustenance of constructivism. The changes we recommend here will force you to keep the emphasis where it belongs: on the learner and learning, rather than on the teacher and teaching.

Clarifying Language Changes

Review the following pivotal words or phrases:

1. **Change "teaching" to "learning."** Force yourself to rephrase every sentence, question, and thought in which you use a form of the words "teach," "teaching," or "teacher" to use a form of the words "learn," "learning," or "learner." Instead of asking yourself how you can teach Johnnie to do long division, change the question to: "What is the best way for Johnnie to *learn* long division?" This forces a shift in your thinking and puts the focus on Johnnie and his abilities, talents, and challenges. This simple, yet not-so-simple, word substitution will generate further questioning and thinking and can lead to a constructivist approach to learning. Remember, you can *teach* students anything, but it doesn't mean they have *learned* a thing.

2. **Change your "lesson plan" to a "student learning plan."** Here again, the idea is to shift the focus from you to the students, from teaching to learning. To change your written plans, especially if you are a new teacher, you may need to create two plans. One will become your agenda—the list of things you will do during the class or day. The other becomes the students' learning plan. It could look something like the plan in Box 4.1. This could be especially helpful for preservice and novice teachers to use as a model student learning plan. Notice that the emphasis is on the student.

3. **Change "cover" to "discover" or "uncover."** Of all the traditional classroom language we hear teachers use, this is the deadliest and the most frustrating. As long as you "cover" curriculum, you won't be able to establish a constructivist learning environment. It's not that content is not important; it is extremely important, but in a constructivist classroom, a teacher does not stand and deliver all or even much of the content. Instead, students uncover, discover, and reflect on content through inquiry, research, and analysis in the context of a problem, critical question, issue, procedure, or theme. Heed the advice and warning of an experienced teacher:

PRESERVICE AND NOVICE TEACHERS:

Box 4.1	
Standard:	*Standard 1A (grades 5-12) (of the National History Standards, for example):*
	"The student understands how the North and South differed and how politics and ideologies led to the Civil War."
Concept:	*Political and ideological differences*
Topic:	*Causes of the Civil War*
Learning Activity:	*Students will work in pairs. Each student in a pair will conduct specific and different research related to the causes of the Civil War. For example, Susie will review newspaper reports of the time period and draw conclusions about the causes of the Civil War; her partner, Sandy, will conduct research on the Internet to determine different viewpoints on the causes of the war. Similarly, other pairs will define their research. [The more different the research assignments are in the different pairs, the more thorough the learning for the whole class.]*
Student Demonstration of Understanding:	*To demonstrate understanding of the causes of the Civil War, students will draw cartoons that analyze the causes*
	OR
	Students will create a video (or skit) that analyzes different perspectives of the causes
	OR
	Students will be involved in . . . [any activity that allows them to demonstrate understanding.]

Covering content or curriculum is like putting a lid on a pot. We shouldn't be putting a lid on the pot; students should be taking the lid off the pot and figuring out what's in it, what it means, and why. (White in Page, 1992, p. 212)

Throwing away the word "cover" has become particularly challenging, but even more necessary, with the advent and pressure of the standards and high-stakes testing movements.

4. **Change "unit" to "investigation" or "exploration."** Can you think of a more boring or inactive word than "unit"? Who could possibly get excited by that word or concept? If you are trying to incorporate active learning into your classroom, you need to get rid of that word and find an action word to take its place. It needs to be a word that conveys in some way the central learning activity. We have suggested "investigation" or "exploration." You can think of others. The trick is to pay attention when you are using the word "unit" and force yourself to make the change. If you put the two words "unit" and "investigation" side by side, what happens in your mind? What would you guess happens in students' minds? Which phrase naturally leads to action? Which phrase makes you think of questioning and problem solving? Which phrase makes you want to do something? Which phrase makes you want to do nothing?

5. **Change "presentations" to "interactive learning experiences."** (Boy, what a mouthful. Can you think of a better phrase to mean the same thing? We'd love to hear from you.) Let's assume you want your students to become active learners who develop their own knowledge. Let's also assume that your students decided to conduct an investigation, carried it out successfully, synthesized and analyzed the new material, drew conclusions, and raised new questions. Those activities would constitute an active learning/constructivist exercise. If you then ask the students to make a presentation based on their learning experience, you will put the class into the position of being receivers of information—just as they would be if you were giving the information. The investigators have had a constructivist experience, but the presentation becomes exactly the type of experience (for the rest of the class) that you are trying to avoid!

PRESERVICE AND NOVICE TEACHERS:

How boring can student presentations be? Very, very boring. Students can learn, nevertheless, just as most educators are having to learn, that there are ways for students to lead learning experiences that actively involve the rest of the class. As long as you call an activity a presentation, though, that's what you will get: a presentation—someone presenting and everyone else receiving. Instead, you can explain to students that they are now the experts in the topic, and their job is to think of an activity that they can conduct with the rest of the class that will allow the class members to be actively involved in learning about the topic.

Although the age of your students will make some difference here, we have seen preservice and novice teachers do this successfully with children who are only in the second grade. One way to develop this sort of task is to ask for the students' ideas on how this could happen. Another is to reflect on components of active learning experiences you develop for the class and figure out how students can learn to use those same components as they develop interactive learning experiences for the class.

Assessing Your Classroom Communication System

Using new language won't cure all the problems of making the shift from a traditional classroom to a constructivist one, but if you don't change your language, you will have a difficult time shifting your thinking. No teacher can speak in a traditional language and expect to have a constructivist classroom. On the other hand, careful consideration of the words you use as a teacher is not enough; it is the entire system of communication that deserves careful reflection. With this in mind, use Checklist 4.2 to assess yourself with respect to the kinds of verbal exchanges one is most likely to hear in your classroom.

✔ CHECKLIST 4.2 The Communication System	4 Always	3 Almost Always	2 Sometimes	1 Never
My classroom communication system is reciprocal rather than teacher directed.				
Students spend more time engaged in their own work than listening to me talk.				
Teacher talk is in the form of critical questions rather than directives.				
If a stranger walked into the room, he/she would be more likely to hear students discussing content than listening to me.				
Questions posed by me or the students don't have a single answer.				
Students feel comfortable asking each other for help in solving academic problems.				
TOTAL SCORE				

Top to Bottom or Side by Side?

Think about the verbal exchanges common in your classroom. In what direction does communication flow?

PRESERVICE AND NOVICE TEACHERS:

It may be more productive in this exercise for you to think back to those verbal exchanges that took place in your classrooms when you were students.

Here's an exchange familiar to many traditional classrooms. When a student asks a teacher about a subject in which the teacher has little background information, a traditional teacher might say, "You don't need to know that." Which of the following might the teacher be communicating here?

1. The information you request will not be part of any future exam constructed by me or the Educational Testing Service.

2. I don't know; therefore, you don't need to know.

3. I don't know, and I am embarrassed to tell you that I don't know (because after all, I am the teacher and I am supposed to know everything).

4. I know everything, including whether or not the information you request is relevant to your life.

TOUGH QUESTION:

? *What if instead of responding "You don't need to know that," the teacher responded with the answer to the question? What would the teacher be communicating to the students about the teacher's role, the students' roles, and the ability of the students?*

In a constructivist classroom, the student/teacher communication system is a **reciprocal** one. For example, in the scenario described above, the teacher might respond, "I don't know. How could we find out?" Students and teachers both initiate classroom dialogue and raise questions. Constructivist communication systems respect the students' abilities to start or add to a discussion and to ask productive questions. In contrast, in traditional classrooms, as Freire (1974) would say, the student/ teacher communication system is a vertical one in which the teacher at the top is responsible for transmitting messages to the students at the bottom. This system sends the message that students cannot figure things out for themselves and that the teacher knows everything.

TOUGH QUESTION:

? *What does this mean: [SM ↔ RM]? (Sless, 1981)*
Hint: It's about communication. Write to us if you cannot figure it out.

Noise

Another aspect of the student/teacher communication system is NOISE. If noise is anything that interferes with a message, then there is more noise (interference) in a traditional classroom communication system than in a constructivist one. The noise in a traditional classroom includes daydreaming, inattention, visual distractions, misunderstandings, boredom, lack of motivation, alienation, and rebellion. In a constructivist communication classroom system, in which the teacher and students are both senders and receivers, both teachers and learners, there is constant clarification, interpretation, and re-creation of messages. This communication system, which leads to student engagement, eliminates most of the noise of a traditional classroom, even though student voices may fill the classroom. How would you describe the noise in your classroom? In what ways can you change the noise to make it dynamic, constructivist noise?

PRESERVICE AND NOVICE TEACHERS: TOUGH QUESTION:

? *How will or do you know when NOISE is productive and when it is not? What will happen if you say to your supervisor, "The noise isn't bothering me at all."? Who is forgotten in that response? When do students need silence in the classroom, if at all?*

Assessing Your Understanding
of Student/Teacher Roles

A constructivist approach to communication is only possible when there is a different understanding about the roles students and teachers assume in the classroom. Take a look at how you view student/teacher roles by completing Checklist 4.3 on the next page.

Don't Give Up Your Responsibility

A constructivist student/teacher communication system does not mean that the teacher gives up responsibility. Although a major role for students in a constructivist classroom is to direct their own learning, they do not have license to do whatever they please. The teacher's role is to guide, focus, suggest, lead, and continually, with the students' assistance, evaluate the progress of the students. Yes, the role of the teacher also is to provide instruction. The question is how much direction, how much intervention, and how much instruction is necessary? As the teacher, you have the experience and the expertise. You also have the responsibility to determine whether or not the learning process is heading to a relevant and academically productive conclusion, and you need to take the necessary steps to ensure that this occurs. Knowing when to step in and redirect is a critical management skill for the constructivist teacher.

CHECKLIST 4.3 Teaching and Learning Roles in My Classroom	4 Always	3 Almost Always	2 Sometimes	1 Never
I have content area expertise.				
I assume responsibility for student learning.				
I encourage students to pose questions and answers.				
Students are curriculum developers.				
Students are responsible for their own learning.				
Students are decision makers.				
Students seek solutions to problems before consulting me.				
I am a facilitator rather than an information dispenser.				
Students pose questions and problems.				
I encourage students to find solutions independently before consulting me.				
TOTAL SCORE				

Teacher/Student Collaboration

In a traditional classroom, you might see a teacher who stands in front of the room, does most of the talking, and tries to fill the heads of her students as if they are so many empty vessels. This is not what we see when we visit—and we visit whenever we can—Jan Carpenter's 1–2 multi-age classroom in Vermont. It takes a few minutes to find Jan. There is no clear front or back of the room, and there is always a quiet buzz of activity. Students are working together around small round tables, or problem solving in a corner of the room, or reading to each other, or sharing ideas about how to solve a puzzle. Many different activities appear to be taking place simultaneously; and Jan . . . well, she's hard to find, but she's in the room. Like her students, Jan is also actively engaged in whatever the class is working on—observing reactions at a science center, talking with students about their plans for a new learning center, or working on the computer with a student trying to solve a math puzzle. Jan sees herself as a learner, and her enthusiasm for learning serves as both a model for and a mirror of the high levels of active engagement taking place in her classroom.

In constructivist classrooms, teachers like Jan see themselves, describe themselves, act, and manage classrooms as collaborators, team leaders, and guides—not as information dispensers, bosses, or disciplinarians. Constructivist teachers ask rather than tell, they model rather than explain, and they work as hard as possible to get out of the limelight so that their students may shine and became independent learners and doers. This means that you will not always direct classroom dialogue; often students will do the initiating. It means that you will no longer be the single, or even the most important, audience when students speak. You will not be the only judge of student work; students will learn to evaluate other student work as well as their own.

The test of your effectiveness will not concern your oratorical skill, your ability to tell a good story, or your ability to prepare a clear and compelling lecture (although you need these skills); nor will it concern your ability to entertain students with scientific discovery, or mathematical prowess, or gripping and bloody tales of historic battles. A good constructivist teacher—in our view, a good teacher—is one who provides opportunities for students to become the great orators, storytellers, historians, mathematicians, and scientists. Students do not become great scientists by listening to the teacher tell them about what great science is; they become great scientists by having the opportunity to *do* science.

Students Who Resist

What about students who like their old roles; or who are more comfortable listening than telling; or who are interested in learning only if it is "on the test"; or who are afraid to try something on their own for fear it is not what the teacher wants; or who find this new approach too much work? If left in traditional settings long enough, students often will balk at opportunities for real decision making and problem solving—after all, it takes more work than simply listening to a teacher tell you what to do, and it can involve more risk. Students may say, "You're the teacher, you tell us!" More outrageously, they may say, "Well, if we have a say, then let's all just do whatever we want, whenever we want." Some teachers view such statements as a call for help, or as an unconscious plea for structure and discipline, or as an example that students cannot be responsible for making good decisions. We see such statements, however, as precious opportunities for class discussion, for group problem solving, and for students to learn how to be independent thinkers and doers. Expect these responses and be ready for them.

PRESERVICE AND NOVICE TEACHERS:

? *How will you respond to parents who complain to the School Board that you are making the students do your work?*

Decision Making in Jan Carpenter's Room

Jan recently introduced a new series of math problems, and she asked the class how they should proceed. One student suggested they break into small groups, another that they choose partners, and a third, Marcy, suggested that Ms. Carpenter present the problems to the class as a whole and that whenever anyone had an idea about how to solve a particular problem, he or she could just call it out. Several students thought Marcy's plan was best and said so.

Jan asked, "How would Marcy's plan work? What do you think would happen if everyone called out an answer at once?" None of the students responded. Jan said, "Let's try Marcy's idea. After all, how will we know if this is a good plan until we try it?" After presenting the first problem, six students called out simultaneously. Jan asked, "What did you say?" In response, the six students repeated their responses but were now joined by several others who sought to help Jan and their classmates. Each tried to speak more loudly than his or her peers. A loud racket ensued. After several moments, Jan asked, "Is this a good plan?" Many students answered, "No." Jan asked, "Why not?" A productive discussion followed, and the class, as a group, arrived at a more useful way of handling the day's work.

TOUGH QUESTION:

?

Neither the constructivist (reciprocal) classroom communication system nor the student/teacher roles in a constructivist classroom translate into a concrete job description for the teacher. Because every activity, every class, and every student is different, how can teachers develop a checklist that will allow them to ensure that the active learning environment will exist or will work?

Assessing Your Classroom
Management and Classroom Environment

Managing a classroom is crucial for developing and sustaining any classroom system, including a constructivist one. If you don't create a safe environment for everyone, your classroom won't be productive, regardless of the teaching/learning approach you follow. What does management in your classroom look like? Complete Checklist 4.4 on the next page before proceeding.

Two components are *critical* to successfully managing any classroom: engaging students in meaningful and relevant active academic tasks and preventing and responding to distracting student behavior in the classroom.

The more engaged that students are in relevant activity, the less disruptive student behavior there will be; the less students are actively engaged, the more disruptive student behavior there will be. This raises some interesting questions for the constructivist classroom. Simply encouraging students to make their own choices does not mean they will automatically become engaged and stay on task. In fact, because they are so used to being in a different kind of classroom system, they may translate your ideas about choice and student directed learning in the following ways:

"Boy, is this teacher weak."

"This teacher doesn't have a clue."

"This will be a ball—we can do whatever we want."

"Yea! There is no teacher."

✓ CHECKLIST 4.4 Classroom Management	4 Always	3 Almost Always	2 Sometimes	1 Never
The classroom is free of daydreaming, inattention, boredom, alienation, and rebellion.				
If I have a concern about a student's behavior, I view it as an opportunity for discussion, resolution, and problem solving.				
Students work together to discuss and create classroom management policies.				
When things fall apart, I take this as an opportunity for the class to discuss solutions to what I and others may see as problematic.				
Students feel safe in my classroom.				
Students understand that there are behavior parameters.				
Students are too engaged in deep learning to be behavior problems.				
			TOTAL SCORE	

Additionally, if you try to make a *revolutionary* rather than an *evolutionary* change in your classroom, most likely you will end up with a classroom in chaos. Do you think this might be what happened to Susan (Chapter 1)? Did she try to do too much that was too different too fast? The change has to be gradual. It has to evolve slowly, with **constant explanation of why you are making the changes** and what you expect. When students feel that the classroom is their room, that decisions about the sequence and scope of their activities are made with their input, classroom management becomes increasingly what its name implies: a method for developing and organizing the complex array of activities that occur in school classrooms, rather than strenuous attempts to discipline, control, or punish students.

In a constructivist classroom, students themselves gradually acquire good management skills when they have the opportunity to practice them.

TOUGH QUESTION:

?

What difference does a seating arrangement make to classroom management?

Little. Changing students' seats may help temporarily. But it does not address the underlying reason for the classroom disruption. Get to the reason for the misbehavior and you can find a more permanent and workable solution.

PRESERVICE AND NOVICE TEACHERS: A SUGGESTION:

A productive way to begin the change to a constructivist classroom and at the same time allow for discussion of classroom management issues is to have students complete the following two statements:

1. The best thing about this class is . . .

AND

2. To make this class better, if I were the teacher I would change . . . because . . .

It is guaranteed that classroom management issues will be embedded throughout the responses. This becomes your launching pad from which you can weave together discussion of classroom management and new approaches to learning.

Assessing Your Understanding of Motivation

Understanding the importance of and how to implement teacher/student roles, a new communication and language system, and how to manage a constructivist classroom isn't enough. What about motivation in the classroom? Does motivation magically happen if you create a constructivist learning environment? Are constructivism and student motivation synonymous? Or is there more you need to think about to put it all together to have the ultimate learning environment? Motivation is a complex and infinite issue. Here we explore what is most pertinent to a constructivist environment and to generating the deepest engagement in learners.

What does Checklist 4.5 tell you about motivation in your classroom?

✔ CHECKLIST 4.5 Motivation	4 Always	3 Almost Always	2 Sometimes	1 Never
I avoid the use of threats of punishment.				
I avoid promising rewards.				
Students pursue topics independently, take initiative, or engage in additional activities related to—but above and beyond—what we are studying.				
Students are disappointed when an activity, lesson, or period ends.				
Students stay late to discuss their work.				
Students look forward to class.				
Students are more concerned with their effort and learning than their grade.				
I develop learning environments with the goal of awakening the students' intrinsic motivation.				
If a visitor enters my classroom, the students pay no attention and continue working.				
Students leave my classroom engaged in conversation about their most recent work.				
			TOTAL SCORE	

Student Choice

One of the ways to explore students' motivational characteristics is to provide an opportunity for choice. In a constructivist classroom, there is often an opportunity for the students to make important choices about what they will study, how they will study it, and how they will demonstrate understanding, for example. But, there is caution needed here: How much choosing the students get to do does not necessarily tell you whether you have a constructivist classroom or activity or whether it's a sensible thing to promote or whether it is even motivating for students. Not done well, it could lead to total anarchy.

TOUGH QUESTIONS:

? *A question of attribution: (Brophy, 1998; Peterson et al., 1997)*
To what or to whom do your students attribute their success or failure? What does this tell you about how to promote success for all students?

PRESERVICE AND NOVICE TEACHERS: TOUGH QUESTIONS:

? *Do your students focus on learning or on grades? Given that research (Dweck, 2000; Kohn, 1993, 1996) shows that students who focus on grades learn less and in less substantial ways, what can you do to ensure that students focus on learning?*

One way to look at the issue of choice is to say: There are times when a student has no choice. This can relate to curriculum requirements, standardized testing, safety issues in the classroom, or a certain book to read. There are times when a student can have total choice. This could be choice of topic related to a bigger theme, choice of research method, choice of demonstration of understanding, or choice of creating a new formula, a new process, or new experiments. There are times when you and the students will decide on things together. This could be the overriding theme, the culminating activity, or the form of assessment.

Again, what is most important in a constructivist classroom can be framed as a question: What are the students doing? Are they figuring something out, trying to create, invent, analyze, or synthesize? Keep in mind that constructivist activities often can be embedded in what appears to be a very traditional framework. Providing opportunities for students to make choices is one small, solid way to begin making changes in your class, and, at the same time, to uncover student interest.

A SUGGESTION:

*If you haven't already read **Punished by Rewards** by Alfie Kohn, you ought to put it on your "to do right away" list. Citing hundreds of research studies to show the negative motivational results of rewards and punishments, Kohn (1993) explains why traditional, behaviorist approaches are so destructive to real learning. Besides asserting that rewards and punishments lead to one person controlling others and are detrimental to positive relationships, he demonstrates that rewards and punishments undermine intrinsic motivation and therefore limit the amount and depth* *of student learning. In a traditional classroom, students become focused on what they will get or what will happen to them when any kind of assessment occurs. They do not focus on what they are learning, why they are learning, and/or why it is important to them. And it is clear from the research that when students focus on some form of evaluation, they lose focus on the learning, learn less, and actually perform less well than if there were no rewards/punishments and all focus was on the learning.*

Scoring the Checklists: Where Are You in Terms of Creating a Constructivist Classroom?

For each of the checklists, count 4 for Always, 3 for Almost Always, 2 for each Sometimes, and 1 for each Never. Put the total score at the bottom of each checklist and then add the scores together. If you scored between 48 (the minimum score) and 80, there is bad news and good news. The bad news is that you have a lot of work to do before your class is constructivist; the good news is that you have nowhere to go but up. If you scored between 80 and 120, you are already making progress toward creating a constructivist class; keep going. If you scored between 120 and 160, you are definitely making strides and probably can use this book to support and confirm what you are already doing. If you scored above 160, give this book to someone else who needs it.

You have just completed a self-assessment. But now, what about assessing student learning, especially in the era of standards and standardized testing?

Standards and Assessment: Back to the Real Basics

Standards: The Elephant in the Room

"Standards," "Grade Level Expectations," "Rubrics," "Benchmarks," "Outcomes," "Adequate Yearly Progress" . . . unless you're living under a rock, it's difficult to avoid being bombarded with these terms on an almost daily basis, particularly if you work in a public school. But what do they all mean? Are they new? Did teachers have standards before the *standards movement*? What is a *standard* anyway? Can one really argue against standards? How can we best measure student progress? Do standardized tests tell us how much students have learned? Do standards require standardization?

Although many in the educational establishment, particularly those who are furthest removed from actually working with students, like to pretend that standards are something entirely new, the truth is that the new *tougher* standards movement is as old as dirt, rearing its ugly head every few years like the cicada after a thankful, but always too short, dormancy. John Holt noted in 1959(!) that an emphasis on higher standards leaves children "too busy to think" (in Kohn, 2004, www.alfiekohn.org/teaching/work shops.htm).

In today's educational climate, questioning publicly the value of the standards movement may seem a little like maintaining that the Earth is flat. How can anyone question seriously the importance of increasing student achievement? Standards help us to: eliminate curricular redundancy, focus on previously neglected content and skills, and clarify what we mean by high expectations. Further, at least historically, standards-based reform is grounded in the idea that:

- active learning fosters in students the greatest command of content;
- people learn best when they are actively involved in problem generating and problem solving; and
- applying concepts and developing and testing theories on one's own is not only powerful, but leads to the most enduring learning.

In addition, standards help us to understand the importance of assessing students' learning in relation to clear benchmarks, rather than in relation to their peers. Standards help students know before an assignment even begins what the expectations are; allow students to monitor their own performance as they work; and provide clear targets to guide students toward continuous self-improvement. In short, standards specify what students should know and how well they should perform in a clear, teacher and student-friendly format. So, what's the problem? This all sounds to be in perfect harmony with constructivism. And it is. But the ways that standards are implemented in our schools is another story. One of our strongest criticisms is the extent to which the movement has discouraged and often prohibited teacher opinion, thought, and questioning.

Asking Critical Questions

Effective teachers face the standards the way they have faced all educational movements and reforms that have come before, by stopping to reflect and to ask critical questions before mindlessly complying with mandates from above. For example, if you teach and use standards, which standards do you use? Did you choose them? Did you have a hand in creating them? Did your students? Why not? Can a teacher create new standards on her own in the beginning of every school year? Teachers rarely have opportunities to explore these questions in public, thoughtful ways. But it is just these sorts of questions that are critical to student learning and active engagement and which must be asked and answered if teachers wish to create learning environments consistent with the propositions of constructivism.

MORE CRITICAL QUESTIONS:

Here are some more critical questions:

- *Is it important that every student, in every grade, in every school in your state (or country!) use the same standards for the same subjects at the same time? Why? Why not?*

- *How does the literature in educational psychology and child development inform us about differing abilities, skills, interests, and desires?*

- *And what about the standards movement's new, tougher, more rigorous expectations? What does rigorous mean? (You may be surprised—look it up in any dictionary.) Many of the state standards (and the new grade-level expectations coming soon to a neighborhood near you) insist that children be expected to master complex materials at increasingly earlier and earlier points in their educational careers. For example, many now advocate introducing algebraic concepts and activities to children in kindergarten. What is the evidence that such approaches are a good idea?*

Both authors of this book earned doctorate degrees and took plenty of advanced mathematics, yet neither had algebra until ninth grade. Would we have been better off taking it earlier? Why? Why Not?

TOUGH QUESTIONS:

In what ways are standards and constructivism incompatible? In what ways are they compatible?

How can students meet standards in a constructivist classroom? How might you demonstrate this to your principal?

What Exactly Are Standards?
Are *Standards* and *Content* Synonymous?

When educators refer to the *standards* or *learning standards*, are they talking about *content*? It depends on what the state and local curriculum frameworks are. Prior to the development and implementation of state learning standard frameworks—although some school districts had no or, at best, vague curriculum policies and documents—the majority of schools typically had curriculum content frameworks. Many schools now have and try to use state learning standards frameworks and school curriculum frameworks simultaneously. The local school curriculum frameworks were and are most commonly lists of content topics that need to be ***covered.*** Likewise, although there are a few state learning standards frameworks which are broadly developed; work with themes rather than specific topics; and encourage and support teacher discretion and choice, the majority of state frameworks also are lists of topics to be ***covered.*** The state frameworks differ from typical local curriculum frameworks in that they contain explicit student performance benchmarks. In any case, whether the words *standards* and *content* are synonymous or not, long lists of required topics to be ***covered*** (whether they are from the state or local frameworks) and in-depth learning are simply incompatible. There is no way the two can be accomplished at the same time.

Content in the Constructivist Classroom

Content learning is one of the most misunderstood dimensions of a constructivist classroom. Traditional teachers, as well as parents, often think there is no connected or even specific content in a constructivist class. This misunderstanding might result from lack of information, or, worse, it might be because content in what a teacher calls a constructivist class has gone awry. Educational reformers often say, "The process is the content." Although they do this to emphasize the importance of problem solving and critical thinking processes, it can lead others to believe that content is not important or that **reformers** think that content is not important. Nothing could be further from the truth in a constructivist class; content is extremely important. The difference between a traditional class and a constructivist class in relation to content is not whether content is important or whether there is content; it is in the way that students interact with, come to learn, and demonstrate their understanding of the content. It is important to know that before you begin to implement any of the models, you need to be clear that you will not be abandoning content.

Two things skew any discussion of curriculum content and/or learning standards. First, it's the deadly word ***cover.*** Even when teachers are in a school system that asks them to develop the curriculum or to align the existing curriculum with the new state frameworks, the questions they raise usually are about what can and should be ***covered*** and when. This is the language with which teachers are familiar. The longer the list of required or recommended topics, the more apt teachers are to feel pressure to teach by telling—to avoid learning experiences that are time-consuming and student driven. Surely teachers' goals do not include burying students in an avalanche of information, but this often is what happens.

Even if good teaching were about ***covering*** content, which it is not, there is no universal agreement on what that content should be. If you get 20 teachers together and ask them what topics students absolutely cannot live without or cannot be considered educated without (at any grade level for any subject), good luck finding agreement. Add parents, school board members, and administrators to this group of teachers and you can expect many deadlocks and disagreements, even shouting matches. If this group does come up with a list, such as a standards framework, it undoubtedly will be a very long one. If you then ask why each of these topics is absolutely essential or how each topic relates to the students' future lives, careers, or to our future citizenry maintaining and creating a better society . . . well, good luck again. Opinions on this matter are like textbooks; unfortunately, everyone seems to have one.

The second thing that thwarts any productive discussion of curriculum content is the definition of curriculum as content. If we can redefine curriculum as ***a plan to engage students in learning,*** we can reframe the complex issues in a positive way. There is no way to develop curriculum content apart from defining teaching and learning approaches without ending up with the traditional boring, inefficient, nonproductive teacher-telling. It happens because the arbitrary mandatory list of topics becomes nonsensically long and impossible to address in any meaningful way. This does not mean that the discussion of necessary and important skill and content/concept learning should not happen. It means that it has to occur simultaneously with a discussion of teaching and learning approaches that promote the most in-depth learning in students.

There is good news and bad news. First the good news: Although many of the new national, state, and professional organization standards frameworks—as explained in Chapter 3—have become more content focused, their core continues to stress the importance of, and advocate for, active student learning. Now for the bad news: As the pressures to prepare students for high-stakes statewide testing place new demands and pressures on students and teachers, teachers feel compelled to violate the very propositions upon which the standards-based movement rests. If you are using a curriculum framework—whether developed by the school, the state, an organization, or teachers—that looks like the table of contents from a traditional textbook, then probably that will become your syllabus, and you will feel pressure to ***cover*** the material, that is, content topics. Again, long lists of required topics and in-depth learning are simply incompatible.

How Can Your Students Meet Standards and Curricula Requirements in a Constructivist Classroom? What Can You Do?

Returning to the Real Basics

Creating a constructivist class is not about lowering standards or losing necessary content. It is not about students having to work less hard than in a traditional class. In fact, when you get back to the real basics, you will discover that the standards are higher, the content is more in-depth, student work is more involved and intense, and student learning is much more comprehensive.

As we said in Chapter 2, the real basics are old. The real basics are not about what you teach (tell) but about how and what students learn. Teacher instruction and student memorization always will be necessary to some degree; the questions are to what degree and in what areas? How can you find the balance? To answer these questions, we need to start with what we know. We know that active learning—that is, when students do their own investigating, figuring out, and creating—is *the* most effective kind of learning. We also know that active learning approaches are time-consuming. That is why you cannot have a long list of content and have much active learning going on. You have heard the "less is more" proposition: That is, with fewer topics, there is greater possibility for rich connections and in-depth learning. Because students do make richer connections and integrate a variety of subjects, the "less is more" approach actually leads to students learning more content, which in turn means that you need to do less teacher telling.

Students need the opportunity to **uncover** the curriculum, not **cover** it. Which do you think is more important and more valuable?

a. Dispensing thousands of bits of information that the student won't remember anyway

OR

b. Having students work on one or a few topics or problems in-depth and develop their own, and sustainable, knowledge and understanding?

Keep in mind as you think about this that in 90 days students forget 90% of everything they have been told (Smilovitz, 1996).

Reviewing Your Own Curriculum Content

There are two important things you need to do to begin to handle the issue of content in a constructivist classroom. First, you have to review your district's curriculum content requirements and state learning standards. If the standards in your state or local school district do, in fact, look like a long list of topics, ask yourself (about each topic) the same thing that students ask: Why do we need to know, study, or do this? If you can't come up with any response besides "because it's required," it's time for you, your department, and your school to rethink the standards or content list or to think about how they can be connected to what is interesting and relevant to your students. Be proactive. Teaching in a democracy is not about accepting mandates without question. Teachers in a democracy, in fact, have a responsibility to constantly question. Be confident in your own ability to recognize what is and is not important for your students.

Making the Mind Shift

Second, you have to believe in student ability. Chapter 6 provides four models that will allow you to address curriculum standards and content while simultaneously focusing on active learning processes for students. None of them will work very well, if at all, if you don't believe in student ability. Here is your chance to assess that belief:

✓ CHECKLIST 5.1 Belief in Student Ability	Agree	Disagree
Students are capable of questioning, investigating, thinking, and discovering for themselves.		
All students can think critically at some level.		
Teachers should help students to become independent thinkers/doers.		
Students need to believe in their own ability.		
Students cannot develop their own meaning or knowledge or perspectives about issues, or learn to make decisions, simply by absorbing the teacher's information.		
A democratic society requires citizens that can think independently.		
Students have the ability to take responsibility for their own learning.		
Students are capable of conducting interviews, publishing their work, writing scripts, and producing TV presentations.		

You have to believe that students are capable of doing great things. If all of your check marks are in the Agree column, you definitely are ready to try some models and probably already have some active learning models of your own. If you have some check marks in the Disagree column, try the simplest model for as long as it takes you to see that students are truly capable of doing surprising things. When you discover this, review this checklist again, then try a model in which you give up more control or in which students do more complex things. The important issue here is this: For students to work with content in a new way, you have to believe they can.

Before you move on to the models, it's time to look at the ugly stepsister to content, curriculum, and standards. Fasten your seatbelts . . . .

The Ugly Stepsister: Assessment

With all of the recent hullabaloo about testing and measuring and evaluating . . . it's easy to forget what assessment is really all about. In fact, at its literal root, *to assess* (from the Latin) means to *sit by*. Although traditional teachers view assessment as distinct from learning (e.g., it is usually conceptualized as the thing we do *to* students *after* they learn), in constructivist terms assessment is, consistent with its etymological origin, more intimate. That is, in constructivist terms, assessment is not something we *do to* students, nor does it occur separately from learning. In fact, assessment in a constructivist class often occurs simultaneously with the learning process.

WHAT'S THE DIFFERENCE BETWEEN ASSESSMENT AND EVALUATION?

__Assessment__ measures what a person is learning and where a person is in relation to expected learning. __Evaluation__ translates that measure into some kind of grade. There are many different forms of assessment including self-assessment, formative assessment (how a person is progressing), summative assessment (the final measure of learning of a particular content or application), and assessment of students by a teacher or others. Often in actual practice, the terms assessment and evaluation are used as if they are synonymous.

Is High-Stakes, Standardized Testing Public Enemy Number 1?

Research in pedagogy long ago established that ongoing, formative assessments by teachers provide the richest, most accurate, most authentic, and most useful educational information. Ask any expert (i.e., teacher) and you will discover that teachers almost never say things like, "Oh, I thought Johnny was a good reader because he summarizes what he reads so eloquently, reads for pleasure, and get excited by books. But since he did poorly on the statewide exam, I guess I was wrong." To make judgments about teachers, students, school districts, and curricula on the basis of one-shot, summative evaluations, as with the current high stakes, standardized tests administered to children who are typically anxious, bored, hostile, or (as they say on the test) "all of the above" is silly.

In the next part of this chapter, we will look at the meaning and purpose of assessment in a constructivist classroom; assessment formats; demonstration of understanding; the good, the bad, and the ugly of rubrics; and quality indicators in a constructivist classroom. But first, complete Checklist 5.2 on the next page.

If you find this checklist difficult or frustrating, you are not alone. For most teachers—preservice, novice, and experienced—assessment is the most complex, most misunderstood, most disliked, most avoided, and most unclear part of a teacher's role.

TOUGH QUESTION:

? *How would you respond to community pressure to increase scores on nationally standardized tests?*

Assessment and Instruction in Constructivist Classrooms

Students may work in large groups, in small teams, in pairs, independently . . . but you will no longer be the sole yardstick by which they will measure their progress. In constructivist classrooms, teachers help students to monitor their own progress, to establish criteria for learning and for quality work, and to devise their own remedial plans. Assessment is not separate from instruction; assessment is a continuous process that drives instruction and is embedded within it (Kugelmass, 1995). Assessment does not bring an end to learning; it provides information about how to continue with respect to learning and curriculum requirements.

✔ CHECKLIST 5.2 Assessment	4 Always	3 Almost Always	2 Sometimes	1 Never
If a student went down the hall to explain what we were working on, why it was important, and what it is like that she has done before, this would not be a problem.				
In my classroom, students participate in creating assessment tools and criteria.				
In my classroom, students know what form the assessment will take before learning experience begins.				
In my classroom, students believe assessment is an opportunity to learn more, not a way to measure one student against another.				
In my classroom, students understand how the assessments we use connect to what we do in class.				
In my classroom, students understand how the assessments we use connect to what we do in class.				
I use assessment to gauge my impact on student learning.				
Assessment tells me as much about my success as a teacher as it does about my students' success as learners.				
I have faith in the ability of students to learn.				
I have a clear philosophy about assessment and evaluation.				
I explain to students that grades are a measure of how much I think they are capable of improving.				
			TOTAL SCORE	

Are Quizzes Constructivist? Taking a Look at Assessment Formats

Traditional assessment formats, such as multiple choice exams, often require students, either through processes of recognition or recall, to indicate what they have memorized. As such, traditional testing formats may be good measures of what students remember and often of how fast they can remember it; rarely, however, are they good measures of what students can do or of what they understand. But they could be. The question to keep in mind is this: What are students doing? Having a test or a quiz in a classroom does not tell you whether the class is constructivist or not. You would have to look at the quiz or test to determine that. Does the quiz or test require student understanding? Does it require that students apply their knowledge? For example: "List the most important rules of capitalization" is a typical traditional test question and does not require understanding. On the other hand, "Create two sentences using two different rules of capitalization and then explain what the rules and uses are in your sentences" requires demonstration of student understanding. Tests and quizzes can be a combination of both traditional and constructivist formats. Using this combination might be a good way to make the transition for students.

Demonstration of Understanding

Ultimately, you should be thinking about assessment as an active demonstration of student understanding and ability to apply this understanding. Think about the assessment process one must undergo to obtain a driver's license. Although a multiple choice exam may be a useful way to assess whether a potential driver remembers the right sequence of steps to parallel park a car, few people would feel comfortable saying that strong performance on such a test indicates good parallel parking ability. To create assessment instruments that do more than merely tap a student's recall or recognition skills, we must reframe assessment so that:

- it is, as much as possible, a continuous process that is part of instruction and not separate from it;
- it connects directly to learning and is introduced before or simultaneously with material;
- it requires students to do more than simply remember (e.g., requires students to develop mathematical formulas, produce exhibitions, write essays, create a sculpture, write poetry, create a musical score, develop and participate in debates, or create and conduct experiments); and so that
- student questions, at least in part, drive the process.

Having described what assessments ideally should look like, we must also keep in mind that there is a danger in becoming too concerned with assessment, per se. The single most important question we should really be asking about testing student learning is not *how* we should be doing assessments but *why* we are doing them. If the answer has less to do with student learning and more to do with making comparative judgments, we're on the wrong track. Speaking directly to teachers, Kohn (1996) suggests:

Ask the students how they can best show you, when we finish . . . what they've understood, what they need help with, what questions they had answered, and what new questions they have. . . . If you are doing grades or tests, make as little a deal about it as possible. The last thing you want to do is talk about good grades as a cause for celebration or stickers. Rather, we'll talk about how it could have been better, how my teaching could have improved, how your learning can improve next week, and then we move on. Otherwise, the grade or the grade substitute becomes the point. (p. 5)

BUT WHAT ABOUT THE SCORES?

This may sound good, but what if the administration of your school is threatening to fire you if your students don't reach certain scores on the high stakes tests? See Chapter 7 and look at the teachers' stories for reassurance. Expect your students' scores to go up.

WHAT ABOUT EVALUATION?

Evaluation is the process of turning your assessment and the students' self-assessments into some form of grade. If you were Alfie Kohn, you would eliminate grades. But in your real life, the school system probably is dictating what the grading system is or can be.

Making changes in your assessment processes requires that you be very clear with your students and their parents what you will be doing and why, and, most important, what your philosophy about learning and assessment is and why. In a traditional system, students come to know assessment and evaluation as punitive. If you have to use grades in your school, then make them mean something different—make them measures of how much a student is capable of improving. That is, a C would mean that the student has much potential for growth. And tell this to the students over and over again.

A Few Words About Rubrics

Seduction and Betrayal

Did you jump on the rubric bandwagon and now wish you could jump off? Are rubrics serving a purpose that makes sense to you? If you are having success with rubrics, you may want to continue using them. You may, in fact, be required to develop and use rubrics by your administrator(s); and rubrics may have some value as part of a teacher's larger bag of tricks. But it is their very ubiquity in educational settings from preschool to graduate school, on tasks as simple as naming colors to tasks as complex as leading a class through a Socratic seminar, that demand more careful scrutiny. They are so omnipresent in fact that rubrics have become the proverbial tail that wags the educational dog. And it is clear why rubrics are so seductive. They promise more teacher control, greater fairness, and explicit, easy-to-communicate expectations. But to a careful observer, it is clear this seduction has a heavy price. For rubrics seduce in many ways, but they also quickly betray. Here are just a few ways rubrics seduce and betray:

The First Deceitful Seduction: Rubrics are more progressive, humanistic, and descriptive than grades.

The Betrayal: A substantial body of educational and psychological research indicates that as students pay increasing attention to *how well* they are doing, they become decreasingly concerned with *what* they are doing. When every discussion, activity, workshop, book read, and writing assignment is evaluated, learning—from a student's perspective—very soon comes to mean one thing and one thing only: measurement. Not, "How is this interesting?" or "What have I learned?" But, instead "How did I do?" By relentlessly emphasizing measurement, we undermine our students' desire to pursue learning beyond what is required for the test, the final grade, or the rubric score. It is why, despite the seduction of a seemingly more humanistic approach, we still so frequently hear, "Do I need to know this for the test?"

The Second Deceitful Seduction: Rubrics allow us to quantify what is truly important. Performance indicators, benchmarks, etc., provide a framework for evaluating everything a student can, should, and may ever do.

The Betrayal: Unfortunately, many teachers have bought hook, line, and sinker the notion that if it's not quantifiable, it's of no value. When in fact in many human interactions, particularly the teaching-learning cycle, the measurable often displaces what is most important. That is, what is most essential is often unquantifiable by its very nature; some aspects of human behavior are lost when we attempt to quantify them. Can we measure student connection, wisdom, excitement, discovery? Is it wise to reduce these things to a number?

NOVICE AND PRESERVICE TEACHERS:

Should all student activities, products, and artifacts be evaluated?
Must everything be measured?

These questions took on even greater urgency for us after we were introduced to some kindergarten teachers in Rhode Island who are now required to create rubrics to evaluate their students' finger painting!

The Third Deceitful Seduction: Rubrics are more objective than grades and offer a more scientifically accurate way to assess learning and understanding.

The Betrayal: Even a cursory inspection of rubrics reveals that there is nothing scientific or objective about them. They still require teacher judgment (a good thing), and often rely for scoring on commonly used terms such as *frequently*, *consistently*, *sometimes*, and *many*. How many is *many*? What do these terms mean? More important, speaking of science, what is the evidence that rubrics deliver on their promise? Is there research that demonstrates the use of rubrics leads to greater student learning and understanding? Perhaps given how commonplace they are, you assume like we did, that the answer to this question is a resounding *yes*. In fact, there is **NO** evidence whatsoever that rubrics accomplish this.

THE TROUBLES WITH RUBRICS:

1. *They are terribly time consuming to develop.*

2. *One of the purposes of rubrics is to keep students from focusing on grades. Problem: Students translate the categories into grades anyway.*

3. *Some students choose a level in the rubric that seems sufficient to them and see no reason to go beyond the minimum.*

4. *Rubrics define for students less than quality work when what is desired is exemplary quality work. Why do this?*

5. *Many rubrics use terms that are meaningless and basically not measurable or definable, such as **most**, **many**, **some**, or **few**. What do these terms mean in any given assignment? Or how about **below standards**, **meets standards**, **above standards**? What do these terms mean?*

6. *THERE IS NO RESEARCH that demonstrates that the use of rubrics leads to greater student learning, understanding, or achievement.*

If not rubrics, then what?

A Better Way: Quality Indicators

A better, simpler, more efficient, and more effective way to clarify expectations and to involve students in assessment at the same time is to codevelop *quality indicators* for each learning experience. It's a simple but very effective process. Let's say you are a second-grade teacher and you have decided to have your students write books about a favorite experience. Ask the students to define what will make these books quality work or the best books. You will be surprised at how clear the students are about what defines quality work. With their ownership in the quality indicators (i.e., standards for the work), they no longer have to be thinking about pleasing a teacher, a process that only produces dependency (not a desirable characteristic in a democracy). As the students write (or produce on computers) their books, they can review the quality indicators listed on large sheets on the wall. These also become the assessment tools, and the students can, in effect, assess their own work. They will need assistance from the teacher in terms of how they assess their own work to understand what meets the quality indicator and what does not. Depending on how much or little experience the students have with measuring their own quality, this can take repeated efforts. In this particular exercise, quality indicators, depending on grade level, can look like this:

All work is neat and easy to read.
There are no spelling or grammar errors.
Illustrations are clear and appropriate.
There is a beginning, middle, and end to the book.

The book is bound in some way.
The book demonstrates understanding of the particular subject area.
The book makes readers think.
The book raises questions for the readers.
The writing is creative and inventive.

This same process works equally well at all grade levels. In our experience, the students appreciate having the input and learning how to assess their own work. Are some students way off in their self-assessment? Yes. These are the students who will need assistance in recognizing how their work matches the quality indicators and how it doesn't. A constructivist teacher has faith in the ability of students and works to make them independent in all areas of learning; and this includes doing at least some of their own assessment.

Five chapters. We've come a long way. We've looked at the definition, historical roots, and supporting research of constructivism; you have also had the chance to complete several checklists as to your constructivist health and to consider the relationship among constructivism, content, learning, quality work, and assessment and evaluation. It's time for you to start thinking about and practicing the *how* of creating a constructivist classroom. In the next chapter, we introduce specific models to help you begin to reframe the way you think about your classroom and allow you to engage students in meaningful learning in the era of standards.

MORE TOUGH QUESTIONS:

1. *In the constructivist classroom, how will you know how much learning the student is doing?*

2. *If discovery is continually reshaped and reinterpreted through teacher intervention, how much learning is really the student's?*

3. *How does a teacher determine if what the student is learning involves erroneous concepts or inappropriate data?*

4. *How can you avoid a situation in which much of a student's search for solutions, new procedures, or conclusions is really the search for what the student thinks is the teacher's right solution or what the teacher is looking for?*

5. *How important are normative, standardized assessments in which a student's performance is compared to other students her age? Are these without any value? Are they really less important than judgments made by you and your students? Is it valuable to know how a student's scores compare with scores from the country, region, state, county, or school? Why? Why not?*

6. *Active learning is time-consuming. How do you accommodate for this?*

7. *How would you respond to a teacher who says, "I will not hand over my teacher-centered approach. Why should I? I've been teaching Greek mythology, or Algebra II, or American History, or . . . (fill in the blank) for 20 years. Of course I know more about these subjects than they do."*

6 Models: Getting Your Feet Wet

Prelude to Implementation:
Preparing Students, Parents, and Administrators

Students and Parents

When you are ready to begin making changes in your classroom, you will first need to handle the explanations for the students. These may take any of several forms but need especially to emphasize that the changes do not mean less work, or abandonment of behavior guidelines in the class, or lessening of standards, or that you are giving up your responsibilities. For parents, communication is essential. They will need a written explanation of changes and how these changes will relate to content topics, standards, standardized testing, and grade formats. Without this clear explanation and reassurance that students will gain, not lose, in their content and skill learning, you will have an ongoing problem on your hands.

Getting Your Principal on Board

The last thing you want to do is alienate your principal. How can you approach the principal so that she is there to support and encourage what you are doing? We surveyed principals all over the country in the three grade groupings—elementary, middle, and high school—and received back questionnaires from New Hampshire, Vermont, Massachusetts, Washington, New Mexico, and Maine. Although we can't generalize from this small, informal survey, we can say that these principals want and need their teachers to:

- speak with them first—arrange a meeting to talk about ideas, obstacles, and concerns;
- be clear about their goals;
- think about how what they will do may affect their colleagues and be prepared for fallout;
- think about how they will respond to parental concerns;
- develop, research (including making school visits), and pilot test their ideas first, preferably within a team or at least with one other colleague;
- be clear about how they will assess learning;

- have clear expectations;
- go slowly; and
- demonstrate success before they become an apostle or complain about traditional methods.

Additionally, these principals give the following advice: Time is crucial; don't waste it. Be ready with a clearly written or oral plan, be ready with supporting evidence, and keep the principal advised of progress or concerns.

When All Else Fails

Although we advocate cooperation with school administrators, it is clear from our experiences—and perhaps your own—that there are times when you will need to go into your classroom, shut the door, and try something you are really convinced will work. We warn you that doing so could be detrimental to your job and general well-being. You can judge this for yourself. If your approach works tell everyone; if it bombs, tell no one.

TOUGH QUESTION:

? *Do you have to become a subversive teacher to accomplish changes? Why? Why not?*

Are You Ready?

Run through Checklist 6.1 and see if you are ready to begin.

✓ CHECKLIST 6.1 Preparation Checklist	Yes	No
I have explained to students why we will be making changes.		
I have explained to students what the changes will be.		
I have explained that changes do not mean students can do anything they want.		
I have written an explanation to parents explaining forthcoming changes.		
I have explained to parents and students how student/ teacher roles will be different.		
I have met with the principal and explained what I will be doing.		

Before getting your feet wet, here are some more tough questions to think about:

MORE TOUGH QUESTIONS:

1. *How will you respond to parents who want less cooperative group work and more teacher dispensing of information or who are concerned that their child is doing all of or not enough of the work?*

2. *How can you assure parents that students are learning not only what they, the parents, think is necessary, but much more?*

3. *How do you get over your own feeling that the "less is more" idea is too narrow a focus and will result in fragmented learning and low scores on the standardized tests?*

If you have looked over the checklists and have made the necessary explanations and preparations with your students, colleagues, parents, and administrators, you are ready to begin. We need to clarify here that there are hundreds of models of active learning that you can try. It is even better when you invent your own models. Remember that if you have not yet made the shift from emphasizing your teaching to emphasizing how students learn, none of these will work very well for you or the students. This chapter will outline four models: Direct Instruction, Where Is the Content?, Group Investigation (GI), and National History Day (NHD). Remember, there is no one road map.

Direct Instruction

PRESERVICE AND NOVICE TEACHERS: TOUGH QUESTION:

? *Does Direct Instruction mean lecture?*

NO, NO, NO, NO, NO!!!!!!!!!!!!!!!!!!!!!!!!!!!!!!!

Direct Instruction is a **process** that involves several steps depending on which version of the model you are using. It is a model that allows novice teachers and preservice teachers in particular to get their feet wet slowly. The overall structure looks traditional; it is actually a structure that good teachers everywhere use. But it is what goes inside the structure that becomes critical. The origin of the Direct Instruction model can be attributed to Madeline Hunter (1982), but long before Hunter developed her printed materials, strong teachers everywhere had the same or similar frameworks for their classrooms. (They didn't know they had millions of dollars at their fingertips.)

We are suggesting the following four-step version of Direct Instruction.

DIRECT INSTRUCTION: TEACHER DIRECTED

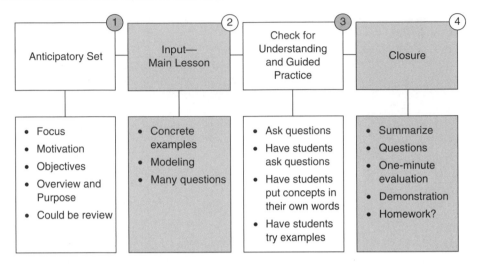

This graphic is fairly self-explanatory and probably familiar. As you can see, this is largely a teacher-directed model. In the first step the teacher provides a focus point. It could be, for example, a critical question on the board, a problem to solve, a list of learning objectives, or a review of previous material. In the second step, the teacher explains a concept and models how to solve connected problems and apply the concept. In step 3, students practice in a variety of ways in order to demonstrate their level of understanding. One way they do this is by applying their new learning. Step 4 is closure.

What we like about this model is that it allows new and preservice teachers to slowly experiment with constructivism by changing any segment of this approach to a more student-driven (as opposed to teacher-directed) learning experience. For example, in step 1, students could create the problem to solve, and in step 2, students could help their peers understand how to solve a student posed problem.

TOUGH QUESTIONS:

?

- *Now it's your turn. If you wanted to "check for understanding" (see step 3 in the graphic) how could you do this in a constructivist way?*

- *How can you make closure constructivist? (Hint: Think student directed.)*

- *Where in this model does assessment occur?*

Because this format looks familiar to both parents and administrators, as well as teachers from their own student days, it is a strong way for novice teachers to begin. When you feel ready to go a step forward, take a look at and try the next model.

Where Is the Content?

Origin and Development of the Model

We call the second model "Where Is the Content?" It is based on the experiences and approach of Eliot Wigginton, founder of Foxfire, which began as a magazine written and produced by students about the oral history of Appalachian people. When Wigginton first started to teach secondary English at a conservative, semiprivate high school in Rabun Gap, Georgia, he found the students to be rebellious, indifferent, and perhaps even somewhat dangerous (e.g., as noted in Chapter 2, they set his lectern on fire when he was lecturing). Realizing that his traditional methods were not working, he asked the students for suggestions of better ways to teach English. (Look at Chapter 11 to see how Susan used this approach.) The result was *Foxfire.*

Students opted to interview local people and wrote about what they had learned. Cultural heritage became the motivating force for learning basic skills. Wigginton assumed that because the students were actively learning and not passively receiving, because there was an audience outside the classroom, and because the students' own interests represented high standards, the students were learning English content and skills. He found support for his effort in the early 1980s when John Puckett spent a year studying the Foxfire program (Puckett, 1986). Through a study of primary and secondary documents, observations, and interviews, Puckett found that compared to results from the boring and ineffective education described by Goodlad (1984) and Sizer (1984) (see Chapter 3), Foxfire's accomplishments were extraordinary, especially in its community and school relationships and in providing students with the opportunity to make decisions and to conduct their own learning.

At about the same time, however, Wigginton began to receive letters of dismay from teachers whose Foxfire programs were not working. These letters led Wigginton to look more closely at his program goals and results. After much reflection, Wigginton realized that producing a magazine had become the main goal for his classes and that publication deadlines had become more important than the educational process. In testing his students, he discovered (Puckett, 1989; Wigginton, 1985) that some knew no more about writing at the end of the year than they had at the beginning, although they had become excellent technicians.

This experience provides an important message for all teachers wanting to try new approaches. Although process skills such as collaborative editing, interviewing, and inquiry are important, they are not enough. **Curriculum content is critical**. As we noted in Chapter 5, saying that "the process is the content" is silly and simplistic. Although the Foxfire model now involves not only writing for magazines but also creating television shows, compact discs, and video tapes, there is a crucial new attention to state and school learning standards.

The Model Steps

To make sure that you and your students meet both state and local learning standards while implementing an active learning approach, try the following steps of the **Where Is the Content?** model:

1. Put the appropriate learning standard(s) on a board, flip chart, or overhead.

2. Start with a very small project. For example:
   - Standard: Students will be able to explain where Saudi Arabia is.
   - Standard: Students will demonstrate understanding of latitude and longitude.

3. Have students brainstorm instructional activities they think will accomplish these objectives.
   - Put ideas on a board, flip chart, or overhead.
   - This exercise will allow students to get started with making choices and decisions about their own learning.

4. Review the activities with students.
   - Do not hand this over to students at this point. If they are not accustomed to doing this, chaos will result. If the students are used to your calling all the shots, keep them feeling safe at this point.
   - Explain to them or ask them (whichever is most comfortable), which activities are possible and which are not, and why. This is not the time for students to be shouting out answers; keep it orderly. **Either they can write down what they think or you can call on them one at a time.**

5. Once you have a list of possible activities, have students decide together on the activities in which the class will engage.

6. Lead and oversee the activities and inform students that you will be doing this.

7. Assess/evaluate learning: Did students demonstrate understanding of the content and skills of the standards?

ASSESSMENT EXAMPLE:

The assessment possibilities will be related to the activities that are chosen by the students.

- *Let's assume the activity involves creating globes. Students are then able to indicate learning by locating Saudi Arabia on that globe.*
- *Let's also assume that the students have painted latitude and longitude lines on their globes. Students can then demonstrate understanding of latitude and longitude by locating cities in Saudi Arabia using only their latitude and longitude measurements.*

OR

- *Students can have input into how the assessment and evaluation will occur.*

WHOA!!! Go directly to constructivist jail. Do not pass GO. Do not collect $100.

TOUGH QUESTION:

> **?** *Do you know what is wrong with these steps???*

The steps to **Where is the Content?** are solid. What needs changing is the order of the steps. Figuring out—with input from the class—what form the assessment will take and what the quality indicators for quality work has to occur either as the first step or as the second step after the target learning standard(s) has (have) been clearly defined and explained. It's punitive to evaluate students after the fact when they have no knowledge of what that is going to look like.

This is a semi-teacher-directed model with student input embedded in the framework. It is the beginning of students learning to be responsible for their own learning. They will have to learn which activities are possible and which are not. Remember, this is not about letting them do whatever they suggest: You have to use common sense here.

Group Investigation

The Basic Model

This model is based on methods proposed by Sharan and Sharan (1989/1990) (see Chapter 2). It is important to note that many cooperative learning methods focus on low-level skills and are simply traditional formats used with groups of students (Slavin, 1989). There is nothing constructivist about such cooperative learning programs. Group Investigation (hereafter referred to as GI), however, focuses on academic achievement and on the development of higher-level thinking skills. This is a group project format in which students work in small groups and gather, analyze, and evaluate data and draw conclusions on a topic of their choosing. They then prepare a report and demonstrate their learning to the whole class. Peers and teachers assess and evaluate the work.

Research on Group Investigation

Research (Sharan & Sharan, 1989/1990, 1992) that compares students in GI classes with those in traditional classes demonstrates that GI students in elementary and secondary schools have a higher level of academic achievement than students in traditional classes. The GI students also do better on questions assessing higher-level learning, although sometimes only just as well on acquiring information. On tests of social interaction, the traditional teaching methods stimulated a great deal of competition among students, whereas the GI method promoted cooperation, mutual assistance, and social interaction among classmates from different ethnic groups.

The Model Steps

Before you get into the steps, you probably will want to have a theme or question on which the class will be working. If the theme or question is related to the learning standards requirements of your grade or class, you do not have to worry about anyone questioning you about where the content is.

ASSESSMENT UP FRONT:

Strange as it may seem, deciding what form assessment and evaluation will take needs to be done up front. Whether you want it to or not, assessment drives instruction. The students can have input here into the form the assessment will take; that is, they will do or create something that will demonstrate their grasp and understanding of the content. They could develop and perform a skit; they could develop and conduct a debate; they could create a documentary. . . .

Once this is decided, the class can then develop the quality indicators as described in Chapter 5.

1. Develop and clarify assessment format and quality indicators.

2. The group decides the topics to be explored. These are topics that would be related to the theme; that is, learning standard(s).
   a. Students brainstorm possible subtopics or subquestions related to the larger theme or standard(s). Questions work the best, but they have to be critical questions—how or why questions—which require and lead to substantial investigation.
   b. Students sort the subtopics or subquestions into categories.
   c. Students form groups by subtopics. If the investigation is at the beginning of the year and you don't know the students very well, a random group selection probably is the best method to use. If you know the students well, you can select the groups according to what you believe will be the most successful organization. If you feel very brave and have worked with groups in this way before, you might try having the students select their own group members. This is the method most likely to fail, so save it for when you are feeling very confident about the method and the students.

PRESERVICE AND NOVICE TEACHERS:

For the sake of your sanity and until you have more experience, select the groups yourself.

3. The groups plan how they will investigate their subtopics or questions. This requires much work on your part. Students need to give you explicit details about how they will conduct their investigation. Students also need to give you explicit

details on what each student in the group will be doing and how each student's part will differ from what the others in the group will be doing.

IF YOU WANT THIS TO FAIL . . .

. . . accept the following statements from the students:

- *We are going to use the Web.*
- *Susie is going to read journals.*
- *Adam will be reading newspapers.*
- *Brian is going to do interviews.*

IF YOU WANT THIS TO SUCCEED . . .

. . . accept the following statements from the students:

- *Susie is going to read the first chapter of Future Shock by Alvin Toffler by Tuesday, March 21.*
- *Brian is going to call Random House Publishers at 1–555–3456 on Tuesday using the phone in the guidance counselor's office and ask how to get in contact with Alvin Toffler. When he finds out this information, he will call Toffler and ask the attached questions.*
- *Adam is going to interview Mr. Conklin and Ms. Boyce on Monday, March 20. This is already set up. The interview questions are attached.*
- *Melissa is going to the school library on Monday afternoon at 3 p.m. and will use the New York Times index to find articles on Alvin Toffler and his book Future Shock.*

Once the students have explicit tasks, you move to the next step, but it is your responsibility to see that these tasks will be productive, possible, and explicit. You may need to have students create additional investigation tasks after they have completed the first tasks.

TOUGH QUESTION:

? *If students make choices as to what they investigate, how can you ensure that there is any unifying thread in your classroom?*

4. Students carry out tasks. Here you need to keep a check on the tasks and their completion. Students need to complete all tasks before moving ahead, and they need to provide you with detailed descriptions of how they will demonstrate task completion. For example:

- Susie will give you a written summary of the chapter she has read and explain in writing what she has *learned* (not what she has *learned about*).
- Brian will give you a written report of his phone conversation with Toffler or a written report of why it couldn't happen.

- Adam will give you a written report of his interviews. He will give the responses and then draw conclusions.
- Melissa will give you a written report of what she found in the *New York Times.*

TOUGH QUESTION:

? *How will you make sure that student groups have equal opportunities for investigation and product development in terms of the resources they need?*

5. Students plan a class learning experience based on their findings (once you are confident the students have done a thorough investigation). Here the details have to be as explicit as they were for the task descriptions. Who will do what? What will be the main experience: A debate? Role playing? A simulation? What will this look like? How will this avoid being merely a "presentation" (see Chapter 4)? And how will it involve the class members?

6. The students conduct their learning experiences, which should demonstrate their understanding; peers will give evaluative feedback to students. Feedback could look like this:
   - The best thing about this learning experience was . . .
   - What would have made it a better learning experience for me is . . .

Assessment

7. You have already set up the form of assessment and the quality indicators. Based on these indicators, students and you evaluate the investigation and each individual's work and input. As a whole, the quality indicators should represent, and ensure that the students meet, the learning standards on which the exercise is focusing. It will take some practice for students to develop a reasonable sense of whether or not other students have reached the quality indicators.

National History Day

Background of Model

If you have survived the first three models, you may be ready for more extensive active learning projects and more time-intensive work on the part of the students. If so, then the National History Day model (NHD) is for you. Although NHD is a national program related to the teaching and learning of history, you can adapt it to any subject area and any grade level. Active learning propositions provide the underpinnings for this program that promotes student competency and interest in carrying out original research in history (this could be in any area) while improving student achievement and critical thinking skills.

More than 700,000 students across the United States participate in this program every year. Students in grades 6 through 12 do the following: select a topic related to an annual theme; find, analyze, interpret, and organize data; relate the data to a historical context; and develop a "presentation" (http://nationalhistoryday.org) on that topic in one of four formats: written research paper, group or individual exhibit, group or individual multimedia documentary, or group or individual dramatic performance (National History Day, Inc., 2004; see also http://nationalhistoryday.org). Students also must prepare an annotated bibliography of primary and secondary sources and write a one- to two-page description of how they researched and developed their presentation and of how their topic relates to the theme. In the official program, which lasts from six to nine months, depending on how successful the students are at district and state judging, the focus is to help students improve their entries. The program culminates in state winners participating at the national level in June at the University of Maryland. Historians, educators, and experienced professionals in related fields judge the entries.

Research on National History Day

A comprehensive study of this program (Page, 1992) suggests the following:

- National History Day provides a method of teaching and learning history that is superior to traditional methods.
- Through participation in the NHD processes, students:
  - learn content, develop in-depth comprehension and awareness of issues, and gain transferable, lifelong skills;
  - gain self-confidence and self-esteem;
  - gain mastery and a feeling of competence;
  - gain a sense of who they are in relation to others; and
  - learn the importance of group and team work and develop cooperative skills.

The Steps

The first thing you need to ask yourself is this: Do you want your process to include judging, as the national program does? This would require that you ask people who have expertise in the discipline area of students' investigations to be judges of the final products. This provides one way to encourage community involvement. You also will have to set up judging criteria. This process could be your assessment approach. It is important to note that the NHD judging process not only allows judges and students to determine the level of analysis and understanding demonstrated through the project but also provides students with suggestions for improving their projects. At each level of judging, except for the final judging at the national program, students are encouraged and expected to make changes in their work. The idea is that learning is not static but vibrant and continuous. Once you have decided on whether to include this judging component, you can begin. Here are the steps to the model:

1. Clarify and define the learning standards or curriculum topic on which these projects will focus.

2. Develop assessment format and quality indicators in relation to learning standards.

ASSESSMENT:

If you decide to use the judging format, the quality indicators are clearly spelled out in the judging pamphlet for NHD. This could be adapted to any discipline area. You can add additional quality indicators as necessary.

If you decide not to use the judging format, then use the approach to assessment in the GI model; that is, work with the class to develop the quality indicators in relation to whatever learning standard(s) and skill development they are working on.

3. NHD provides a particular theme each year. You could decide to use their theme as adapted to your discipline area. If you do not use the NHD theme you, or you and your students, select a broad theme or topic related to required learning standards. Themes that you could use in any content area and in relation to many learning standards would be something like:

   - Rights and Responsibilities
   - The Individual in Society
   - Conflict and Compromise
   - Triumph and Tragedy

Or you could choose something that might be the title of a section in your textbook or out of a specific required curriculum:

   - Light
   - Immigration
   - Percentages
   - Metaphors
   - Neighborhoods

Or you could choose something very limited so that this project would be small. As small as you might think a project is, a project can take on a life of its own.

4. Students and you define subtopics or subquestions as in the GI model. Students can brainstorm possible subtopics or questions and then come to agreement on five or six of the most promising. Possible subtopics might be:

   - What were the rights and responsibilities of the Irish immigrants in the early 1900s?
   - What are the rights and responsibilities of pharmaceutical companies in developing new drugs?
   - How can metaphors be used to define conflict?

5. Students form groups (or work as individuals). Use judgment again. If you are new at this and students are going to be working in groups, you decide group memberships; if you have a great deal of experience, do what works best for you.

6. Students in groups discuss how to investigate the issue or subtopic, and each group member defines his/her tasks. **Step 2 of the GI model applies here**, regarding students' plans for how to investigate their topic and specific tasks to be performed. If these task definitions are not explicit, this procedure will fail. For example, if the theme were immigration, promising task definitions might include the following:

   • Jared will go to the school library tomorrow afternoon to find articles from the *New York Times Index* for 1920.
   • Sean will interview his grandfather, an immigrant from Ireland, on Tuesday night.
   • On Wednesday Sheila will go to the school library, set up the copy stand, and take photos from the *National Geographic* issue on immigration from February 1918.

7. Students decide what format they will use for the final product. As explained briefly above, in the NHD model there are four possibilities for how students can demonstrate their understanding and analysis of their topic:

   • Written paper—only individuals can select this.
   • Group or individual dramatic performance—this requires doing the research; writing a script that demonstrates understanding, analysis, and mastery of the topic; and performing the script in 10 minutes or less.
   • Group or individual multimedia documentary—this requires the same kind of research, writing a script, and then developing a media production that demonstrates understanding, analysis, and mastery of topic. This documentary cannot be longer than 10 minutes. This time limit requires students to condense, synthesize, and demonstrate understanding of the most important concepts. The possibilities are endless and include drawings on overheads with analysis on audiotape, a slide show with audio tape analysis, a PowerPoint documentary, a videotape production, a computer-aided demonstration, and Internet possibilities.
   • Group or individual exhibit—requires the same as above except that students demonstrate analysis and understanding through a stand-up project with specific size and word limitations: no taller than 6 feet, no wider than 40 inches, no deeper than 30 inches, and no more than 500 words (National History Day, Inc., 2004).

8. Students conduct the research or investigation. The scope of the project determines how long this will take: as little as one class period in your school or as long as the school year. Follow GI steps here.

9. Check and recheck. This is where you monitor the reports from students on their investigation tasks. This is ongoing and allows you and the students to progress in a productive direction.

10. Students prepare an annotated bibliography of their work. (Yes, students in the sixth and even the third grade can do this.)

BIBLIOGRAPHY MODEL:

A workable model for all grades is for students to list bibliographical entries, with each entry followed by two sentences. The first sentence explains the content of the source. The second sentence explains specifically how it was of value (specifically) in this research (i.e., "We used this source to determine percentages of Irish immigrants landing in the port of Boston on July 15, 1909.").

11. Students compile, interpret, and synthesize their material (photos, scripts, etc.).

12. Students prepare the demonstration and write a one- to two-page report per group on:

   - how their subtopic relates to the theme;
   - how they conducted the research; and
   - how they developed the demonstration or product.

13. Students demonstrate their understanding, skills, and product.

Judging Format

If you have decided to use the judging format, here are some guidelines you might want to follow.

Judging

1. Select three judges.

2. Judges review each annotated bibliography and then ask students questions about their product or demonstration (five minutes maximum, because the product should be able to stand alone). This conversation is to determine if students have done the research themselves and understand the concepts and significance of the topic.

Scoring

1. 60% of Score: Content Quality

   - Is the content accurate?
   - Is there analysis and interpretation of content rather than just a description?
   - Do the students demonstrate understanding?
   - Does the annotated bibliography demonstrate wide use of available sources?
   - Were primary sources used?

Questions judges could ask to help determine score:

   - What was your most important source and why?
   - Why did you choose this category for your topic?
   - What is the most important point you are trying to convey about your topic?
   - What is the most important thing that you learned from completing this project?

2. 20% of Score: Demonstration Quality

- Is the entry original, creative, and imaginative in subject and implementation?
- Is all written material clear, grammatically correct, and correctly spelled?
- Does content display a measure of literary style?
- Is all visual material clear and appropriate?
- Do students display adequate familiarity with their equipment?
- Is acting of accomplished quality?

3. 20% of Score: Adherence to Theme and Rules

- Does the project focus on the theme or main topic?
- Does the project demonstrate the significance of the subtopic in relation to theme or main topic?
- Is the theme handled in a unique way?
- Did students operate all equipment?
- Did students create all parts of the project?
- Did students complete the demonstration in 10 minutes or less? (Automatic five-point deduction if not.)

Tabletop projects do not have time limits but have size limitations (see p. 71).

ASSESSMENT:

If you use the judging format, you have already done the assessment planning as long as quality indicators in relation to the learning standards are addressed. Now just assess.

If you are not going to use the judging format, then you use the quality indicators developed by you and the class as the measures of learning.

AVOIDING PRESENTATIONS:

To make this complex constructivist experience work to its fullest, provide and require a way for students to change from "presenting" their work to leading a learning experience for the whole class in which the class members are involved in their own learning of the topic (see Chapter 4).

Teacher Reflection

Each time you implement one of these models, you need to reflect on successes and problems. This will allow you to make adjustments for your classes for the next time you implement a model. Checklist 6.2 is a Reflection Checklist that is self-explanatory. It would probably be most useful if you stick with one model until most of your responses are in the "Yes" column.

✓ CHECKLIST 6.2	First Time		Second Time		Third Time	
	Yes	No	Yes	No	Yes	No
Students were totally involved.						
Students understood what they were doing and why.						
Students liked the new approach.						
Students were able to demonstrate understanding.						
I felt comfortable doing this.						
This was the hardest thing I've ever done.						
I want to do this again.						
I was thrilled by the students' engagement.						
I was organized and clear about what I was doing.						
I saw tremendous improvement in students' work and comprehension.						

Although some readers may want to stick to these models for a while, others with more teaching experience may be ready for more complex constructivist approaches. In the next chapter, we discuss issues pertinent to the various grade levels and present teachers who describe models—including interdisciplinary team investigations, student-developed curricula, and theme-based programs—that are even more constructivist in nature than those described in this chapter. These teachers will introduce you to their procedures, successes, and concerns.

We will finish this chapter with more Tough Questions and two challenges:

MORE TOUGH QUESTIONS:

1. How can you use these models in sequential subject areas such as math and foreign languages?

2. How will you handle parents who say that this is way too much work and is interfering with family life?

3. How will you handle parents who try to do part of the students' work on these projects?

TWO CHALLENGES:

A new teacher, Dave Antonio, introduced the National History Day model to his high school biology class. The theme was composting. There was a requirement that students demonstrate understanding of composting through some form of technology. Dave explained, "While their projects were extremely diverse, the students spent more time learning about technology than about composting. This was valuable, but I felt they lost the focus of the topic." **What would you do to avoid this happening in your class?**

When Rachel Marsh introduced Group Investigation processes to her sixth-grade students, they seemed excited. The students, however, did not seem able to work cooperatively in groups. **What would you do to prepare students for the GI processes to avoid this problem?**

Diving In: Teachers Tell Their Stories

We were studying ancient Greece. Students had researched a particular person of the time and came prepared to enter into dialogue as that person. One minute before class, my department chairperson, who had been hearing all of these stories about my unorthodoxy, announced that he was going to sit in on the class. So we began. The students really got into it as I asked Alcibiades, Zeno, and Aristotle what they thought about various topics and about the comments of Socrates. Students were going crazy jumping in with comments and questions, while staying in their roles. After class, I got no comment from the Chair so I asked him for a reaction, "You've got some very good students there. You do teach the political facts, though, don't you?" he replied. (D. Christensen, personal communication, January 31, 1997)

How do real teachers get back to the *real basics?* How do they set up classrooms to allow for and encourage active learning? How do they handle the unique challenges that constructivist classrooms and their grade levels present? How do they deal with administrators, parents, school board members, and other teachers who simply don't get it? In this chapter, you will meet teachers at the elementary, middle, and secondary levels, and you will hear what they have done, what challenges they face and have faced, and what issues they have had to address. More important, you will see how they have developed their own styles and models for creating and sustaining their constructivist classrooms.

In the first part of this chapter, we will introduce new readers to the three teachers we featured in our first edition. This section will also feature sections that define the issues relevant to the K–4, 5–8, and 9–12 grade levels. In the second part of the chapter, three new teachers relate how they have created and sustained constructivist approaches for their students in times of the standards movement, standardized testing, and the No Child Left Behind Act (NCL B) of 2001.

Elementary School: Leaving Home for the Bigger World (Grades K–4)

A primary issue for elementary teachers is how to develop experiences that will allow our youngest students, many of whom have not yet cut their second set of teeth, to interact with, integrate, and understand what seems like vast amounts of new information. For many of these teachers, approaches that emphasize student-directed, active learning are old hat. For too many others, this concept could not be more foreign. When we visit local elementary schools, we are often struck by the number of teachers who use lecterns(!); who spend more time talking, telling, and instructing than listening, guiding, and facilitating learning; and who break content learning into regimented time blocks as if, for example, students could only learn math between 9:20 a.m. and 9:42 a.m. On one recent visit, we observed a third-grade classroom in which the teacher's blackboard contained the following information:

Spelling—8:12–8:37
Language Arts—8:37–9:02
Reading—9:02–9:27

We didn't read to the bottom of the board: The first three lines were perfectly clear. In this room, the teacher views and introduces even closely related subjects as separate from one another; the teacher presents new information every day, in the same order, in the same way.

PRESERVICE AND NOVICE TEACHERS:

When a volunteer parent comes to your first-grade classroom and is concerned that the students, not you, are leading Calendar Time, what will you do?

As noted in Chapter 5, the way one views the curriculum drives teaching and learning. If you view language arts, spelling, and reading as distinct from one another, you will tend to convert opportunities for the *learning* of language, spelling, or reading into preset time schedules for the *teaching* of language, spelling, or reading. Even if you don't think this way, administrators often make the kinds of curriculum decisions that require you to break *learning* into *teaching* segments. Many teachers feel compelled to follow along. The teacher you are about to meet describes quite a different approach to student learning.

WHAT IS CURRICULUM?

IT IS: A plan and way to engage students in learning. Curriculum is everything that happens in your classroom.

WHAT IS CURRICULUM NOT?

IT IS NOT: A list of content topics to be covered in a certain time frame.

Meet Jan Carpenter

"Jan Carpenter" (a pseudonym), is an experienced teacher in a multi-age 2–3 classroom in a community of lower socioeconomic level outside Burlington, Vermont.

Jan's Mind Shift

Several years ago, after teaching for 13 years, I began gradually to change the way I perceived children as learners. Instead of looking at children as glasses waiting to be filled, I saw them as fires waiting to be ignited. I realized that children were naturally curious about the world around them and were constantly formulating ideas to explain their discoveries. And I came to see that if they had meaningful and interesting activities with enough time for exploration and validation they would develop true understanding. While a traditional approach often suited my needs as a teacher, it did little for my students.

. . . what had the most profound impact on my teaching approach was participation in the Vermont Elementary Science Project. This gave me opportunities to experience inquiry science. I learned how to collect, organize, analyze, test, and apply evidence. I knew that was the approach I wanted for my students. My role as teacher changed drastically. I became a facilitator. I no longer stood in front of the class disseminating information. I set up activities that would help build on students' prior knowledge or understanding of a concept. This approach, which started from student interest . . . allowed me to integrate other subject areas in learning activities.

Jan's Process

Even though I was focused on science, I developed a program that integrated science, math, and language arts. Why? Two reasons: First, learning is not done in isolation; it is interconnected. For example, how can you possibly learn about light without figuring out angles? Second, integration provides the most precious gift a teacher can receive—time. It took a few years before my science, math, and language arts program truly reflected my beliefs. Here is my approach now.

First stage. In the first stage, I provide opportunities for students to become actively curious about our topic. I create this invitation in various ways: New objects to explore and to explore with, observations of the natural world, or a problem to be solved might promote active inquiry in this stage. Students start to ask: "What is this?" "What does it do?" "What do I already know about this?"

Second stage. In the next stage, students explore and discover. They begin by "messing around" with the materials. This focused play gets the students ready for more in-depth observations. Students can't make detailed observations until they've had an opportunity to engage in free exploration of materials. For example, if students have never seen or used a light box, you can't expect them initially to use it to gather information about light. Their fascination with it would prohibit these discoveries until they had time to explore its superficial features.

After students spend an appropriate amount of time exploring, a stimulating or productive question will create an invitation to take a closer look or to encourage a new investigation. These questions ask children to show rather than to say answers. Many begin with "How . . ." or "Why do you think. . . ." Throughout this phase, students are recording observations and ideas. Students are talking with each other. They are sharing, discussing, debating, and discovering.

To integrate technology into the learning, I present the following design technology challenges:

- *Design Technology Challenge #1: Build a functioning lighthouse that is at least 16 inches high and that allows light to be seen from all angles. (Materials: poster board, wood from the linx kits, clear cups, glue, wire, flashlight bulbs, D batteries)*
- *Design Technology Challenge #2: Build the most inexpensive device that can be used to search for things lost in the dark. (Materials: wood, poster board, Dixie cups, D batteries, flashlight bulbs, wire, tape)*

Third stage. The third stage involves students communicating their explanations and solutions. This reporting out time is similar to a scientific convention. Students present the evidence they have acquired during their investigations via charts, diagrams, and drawings. This gives students the opportunity to demonstrate their understanding of the concept or skill.

PRESERVICE AND NOVICE TEACHERS:

How will you respond to the parents of your third-grade students when they complain to you: "Elissa, Joel, Rana . . . already studied Native Americans in the first and second grades. Why are they doing it again?"

What If You Are Not Jan Carpenter?

Jan Carpenter, as explained above, is an experienced teacher and reached this level of success after five or six years of working with and adjusting the procedures and steps. The first time you try any constructivist approaches, you probably will have a mixture of successes and problems. This is why reflection is so essential at the end of each attempt. Each subsequent time you try the approach, you will have ironed out some of the things that didn't work. In the next section, after looking at the main issues at the middle school level, you will meet two middle-level teachers who had much success in implementing a constructivist-based, student-developed curriculum but realized they would need to revise the process the next time around.

PRESERVICE AND NOVICE TEACHERS:

What will you do when a parent of one of your fourth-grade students goes to the principal to demand that students in your class learn the multiplication tables the way she/he did rather than learning math through problem generating and solving?

UPDATE ON JAN CARPENTER:

As the implementation of the NCLB and standardized testing movements bore down on Jan's school, her principal required that all teachers post the students' standardized test scores (not by individual name) outside their rooms for all to see. As offended by this order as Jan was, she relented and did it. She did not, however, change at all her constructivist classroom and approaches.

The principal was incensed when she realized that Jan's students' scores were higher than the scores of other teachers—especially since the other teachers were traditional teachers or had reverted to traditional approaches, including teaching to the test to enhance (or so they thought) test scores.

Middle School: If You Don't Know or Remember What Young Adolescents Are About, You Will Wish You Did (Grades 5–8)

Young Adolescent Needs

Between the ages of 10 and 14, students will change more rapidly and pose more divergent issues for their teachers than at any other time in life except infancy. It is in these grades where we first begin to lose students to the educational system. According to *Turning Points,* the middle grades "are potentially society's most powerful force to recapture millions of youth adrift, and help every young person thrive during early adolescence" (Carnegie Council on Adolescent Development, 1989, p. 8). Although some students are beginning to make a transition from concrete reasoning to abstract thinking, most middle school students are still operating at a concrete thinking level. This means that they learn best when involved in a real problem. This fits with the concepts of constructivism—that is, that the longest-lasting and deepest learning occurs when it occurs in context.

Physically, middle-grade students have as wide a range in development as in cognitive development. The young women can mature physically two years before the young men. Students may appear awkward or gawky and be very uncomfortable sitting for long periods of time because bone growth can exceed muscle development. Besides the cognitive and physical changes, there are emotional and social changes. The most crucial search of their lives—Who am I? How do I compare to others?—begins at this age. Friends and peer groups and belonging become increasingly important to young adolescents. These characteristics and needs need to be at the core of your constructivist approaches.

Organizational Features of Reformed Middle Schools

In the 1990s, many, many junior high schools took up the rallying cry of the *Turning Points* (1989) Carnegie research and recommendations. It is why you rarely now see *junior high* schools; instead the schools have become *middle schools* with configurations ranging from grades 5–8 to 7–9. For some of these schools, there were no substantial changes other than the name; for others, changes were dramatic. Some of you probably are already familiar with organizational features recommended in *Turning Points* to enhance the learning experiences of middle schoolers. Two of the most prominent recommended features were interdisciplinary teaming and block scheduling.

The rationale behind **interdisciplinary teaming** or partnering was to allow teachers to work with each other in flexible time periods to best meet the learning needs of students as well as to get to know students better and to let students feel as if they belong. **Block scheduling**, which was developed (although this was kept somewhat secretive) for the purpose of forcing teachers to create and use constructivist approaches, complements the interdisciplinary format. It allows teachers in the team or partnership to decide, for example, that on a certain day the students need longer to investigate a science problem. This longer time period is meant to allow for, and support, the active learning approaches of constructivism. It also allows integration of subject matter. For example, on Monday students might spend a two-hour block of time on science experiments; and on Tuesday they might spend a two-hour block on solving math problems connected to the science experiments, or the math and science teachers on the team might work together for the total of four hours and integrate the material and tasks for both days.

Effects of the New Mandates

As the standards and standardized testing movements have infiltrated the system of schooling some, and in some cases many, of these middle school reform concepts and practices have fallen by the wayside. The emphasis has returned to content coverage and scores on tests. Many teachers have left the profession because of these pressures; many have stayed and are living unhappily with the mandates. It doesn't have to be one way or the other. You have the power to make your classroom a constructivist classroom, an active learning classroom, and a successful classroom regardless of any mandate that comes down the road. (Meet Matt, Marie, and Don in the second half of this chapter.)

Students Developing Their Own Curriculum

At the most progressive end of the constructivist continuum are the schools in which students not only construct their own knowledge through active learning processes but also play a major role in developing their own curriculum. Although this is not as common a component of middle schools as interdisciplinary teaming, for example, it will be to your advantage to understand the possibilities of this approach. Questions about themselves and their world generate themes that students investigate throughout the year (Beane, 1993; Brodhagen, Weilbacher, & Beane, 1992). The investigations typically include all the major subject areas in an integrated fashion and align with state standards. At the Williston Central School of

Williston, Vermont (Burrello, Burrello, & Winninger, 1995), which is probably one of the most progressive and most constructivist middle schools in the nation, students in multi-age (grades 5–8) groupings define and develop much of their curriculum.

Don't Forget the Content

Parents can get very concerned when they don't see evidence of, or can't find in their students' work, the appropriate learning standard and topics. They will question how their children will be ready for high school if they are not addressing this content. They have every right to be concerned, not so much in relation to whether students will be prepared for high school (there are many things that need to change in the high schools) but because content is a major piece of education and learning. If you cannot show or explain where and what the content is and how it is not the same as the content of last year or the year before, something is wrong. You may be paying too much attention to the process and not enough to the "beef." This is so whether you are working alone or with team members in interdisciplinary approaches.

MANAGING THE STANDARDS:

At the Williston Middle School in Williston, Vermont, students work with a computer program developed specifically for that school. The program contains all of the learning standards that students need to meet in all discipline areas for grades 5–8. Students then control their own destiny with the help of their facilitator who meets regularly with each student to determine what standards the student has already met and how and on what standards the student is currently working. Students present proposals to their facilitators indicating which standards they will focus on and how they plan to meet them.

Keeping Track, Grading, and Communicating

Parents need to have clear explanations of how you and students keep track of their work; additionally, they can have major issues about grades and grading systems with which they have had no experience. An increasingly common grading practice at many middle schools that support constructivist propositions involves students developing the criteria for assessing their own work. At Vermont's Williston Central School, students develop quality indicators for every project or piece of work (see Chapter 5). When the indicators the students suggest are either not valid or simply are not attainable, the facilitator helps to redirect the students in developing more productive kinds of indicators. The more the students practice self-assessment with the facilitator's assistance and feedback, the sooner they become expert at evaluating their own work in relation to a high standard.

Meet Ann Lipsitt and Janette Roberts

Ann is a seventh- and eighth-grade special educator, and Janette is a language arts/ social studies teacher in the eighth grade at Browns River Middle School, about 25 miles from Burlington, Vermont. A large percentage of the students at Browns River come from professional families. There are about 500 students in grades 5–8. Ann and Janette, who had recently completed a course that focused on instruction and curriculum in the middle grades, decided to involve their students in developing part of the curriculum. In this project, Ann and Janette tried to address the issue of young adolescent identity search, to incorporate recommended organizational features described above such as block scheduling and interdisciplinary partnering, and to involve the students in self-assessment.

Ann and Janette's Process

You're probably thinking the idea of student-developed curriculum—a process in which students generate questions about themselves and their world and then choose related themes to investigate—sounds nice, but how does it work really in a classroom of 24–25 students and on a middle school team? Our team includes 50 students, the two of us, and a variety of auxiliary personnel who assist with students with special issues or disabilities. The topic for our project was immigration and industrialization in the United States during the late 1800s to early 1900s, a time period mandated by the district's history curriculum and learning standards.

Engaging the Students

To get our students actively involved in understanding the impact of industrialization and immigration on life in the 19th century, we did three things. First, we went to a local museum where each of us (yes, the students, too) assumed a role typical of the time period. Everyone experienced life in the 1800s as a person living in a rural environment among an extended family. Students worked with farm animals, prepared a complete meal, performed household chores, quilted, and discussed issues of the times as they performed their jobs. Next, students wrote reaction papers which addressed how they felt about the experience and what they learned. And finally back in the classroom, the students read at least one novel to extend their understanding of the time period and to broaden their interest of the topics they were studying.

Developing the Curriculum

After a week of reading, each student designed a character and assigned him- or herself a role determining whether he or she would be a farmer, immigrant, mill worker, working child, or possibly an overseer. Each student developed a character and made up a life story for this person using the information he or she had learned. As students wrote about their characters, they also made lists of interests, problems, and questions they would have experienced and had in their daily lives. This not only engaged the students, but allowed them to tap into the deep issue of "Who Am I?" Their own issues came out through their characters' issues. From these lists of concerns, questions, and issues, the students developed broader topics or themes. Using large pieces of newsprint, we wrote their themes and topics down for future reference. These lists remained on the walls throughout this project. There were 14 themes/topics ranging from Irish immigration to labor reform.

Each student received a typed copy of the lists. Together, we generated specific questions we might want to answer about each topic/theme. We came up with a list of almost 50 questions. As the list grew so did the students' interest. The questions included: "How did immigration impact Americans?" "Why didn't everyone get the same education?" and "How was the world reacting to successes in America?"

Brainstorming Activities

After developing the questions, students brainstormed activities that could be used to find answers and other activities that could demonstrate their knowledge and understanding of the questions. It still delights us that the students created a list of possible activities that was uncannily similar to the one we created in anticipation of this process. For obtaining the information, the students came up with:

- *Inviting guest speakers to classroom*
- *Watching videos and documentaries*
- *Writing, calling, or using e-mail for information from Ellis Island, Sheldon Museum, Shelburne Museum, the Vermont Historical Society, local historical societies, and the Vermont Folklife Center*
- *Interviewing local people to obtain oral histories*
- *Using school, local college, and regional libraries*
- *Taking field trips to museums and local mills*
- *Researching local records at town offices*
- *Getting information from the World Wide Web*
- *Reading biographies and historical fiction*

And for demonstrating understanding and knowledge [grasp of content], they thought of:

- *Building a scale model*
- *Doing a painting or mural*
- *Making a collage*
- *Writing and performing a song*
- *Creating games*
- *Making puzzle books*
- *Writing a typical cookbook*
- *Preparing typical foods*
- *Making and demonstrating crafts*

- *Producing a video*
- *Creating a presentation*
- *Producing multimedia presentations*
- *Creating a music video*
- *Preparing wax museum pieces*
- *Writing and performing a skit or play*
- *Creating advertising brochures*
- *Making posters*
- *Developing a simulation*
- *Role-playing*
- *Creating a time line*
- *Writing a newspaper*
- *Constructing a public display*
- *Preparing a flip book or pop-up book*
- *Writing a research paper*
- *Retelling stories of the time period*
- *Creating inventions using materials and tools of the time period*

Investigating

Next, students chose topics for investigation. We asked a variety of questions to help students pick topics of interest to them. We made judgment calls about what were reasonable choices and productive learning experiences. Some ideas that kids came up with needed to be discarded or significantly revised, For example, one student decided she wanted to study women in the labor movement. Unfortunately, the topic became overwhelming and she found herself floundering among the information and the number of events that were occurring at that time. Through our questioning, she was able to narrow her topic to the Triangle Factory fire, which allowed her to study the women's movement within a particular framework.

Negotiating Assessment

Before the investigations began, together with the students we developed a rubric to define quality work. This was done fairly easily as the students had been working on rubric development all year. Students also observed and analyzed models of excellent and poor quality work so that they could understand what makes a product effective or ineffective. The students decided they wanted to share their work with a wider audience, so together we designed the culminating day to include historically accurate games, dressing up in time-period costumes, and creating a potluck meal. All of this was decided before the research began.

Working in Block Time

In addition to working outside of the classroom, students had 80-minute work periods three times a week for three weeks to do research and develop a project. At the end of each block time, students wrote a journal entry with the follow specific items:

- *What did I accomplish?*
- *What resources did I use?*
- *What is my plan for the next scheduled block time?*
- *What materials do I need next?*
- *What problems am I having?*

All responses had to be detailed and specific. This was difficult for students who were not used to being specific, so we created a model of a detailed journal and made overheads of exemplary journal entries.

TWO CHALLENGES:

Sean and Yurij, middle school teachers in a rural mid-western area, introduced a student-developed curriculum process to their fifth-grade students. After the students had made lists of questions they had about themselves and their world, they decided their theme for investigations would be "death." This was a combined social studies and language arts interdisciplinary exploration. Although Sean and Yurij were amazed by the results and how much the students learned about themselves and others, some parents disapproved of the project. One parent even threatened to take Sean and Yuri before the superintendent if they continued with the project. What do you think happened here, given this brief scenario? What would you do to avoid this happening in your classroom?

A new teacher, Phil Stevens, tried working with a student-developed curriculum. On the positive side, he found that students were actively involved and interested, they had grasped major issues, and they had learned an area of interest in depth. However, he also found that the following were problems: keeping track of who was doing what and when, finding materials, students turning in poor quality work, and students dis-respecting each other's work. If you wanted to try a student-developed curriculum, how would you avoid these problems?

Results

Successes

We believe that the students learned more about this time period than we could ever have possibly "covered." Everyone learned how to be a researcher, how to ask good leading questions, how to look at cause and relationships from a historical perspective, how to manage time, and how to organize and orchestrate a project from initial questions to conclusions. And most of all, everyone learned what living in the 19th century might have been like. They also developed a better understanding of how past events affect our lives today. Because they generated the questions and searched to find the answers to their own questions, we believe they are more likely to remember this learning experience. And, because so much of the investigation was done by the individual learners themselves, we believe that they have mastered many of the skills necessary for continuing to generate questions and to know how to locate answers and find solutions, not only from textbooks and authority figures, but from a whole host of other sources as well.

When we asked students to reflect on this learning experience, almost all of them stated that they appreciated and liked having the opportunity to make choices about what to learn and how to demonstrate what they had learned. The most positive and numerous response was that they had a lot of fun during the culminating day's activities.

Problems

Initially everything did not run smoothly. Lots of students needed guidance and direction. They wanted us to tell them what they should do, and it was tempting to give them our ideas. One of the biggest problems was knowing when and when not to intercede. For example, one group of self-directed students wanted to create a cookbook and menu—everyone would sign up and bring in a dish they had researched and determined appropriate to the time period. This sounded reasonable until we looked at the list of dishes they were selecting. We knew that few families would have the ingredients necessary to make some of the highly unusual ethnic dishes which they had selected. A compromise was finally reached when we agreed on a luncheon meal that included a variety of pastas and ethnically diverse desserts—typical dishes made by family members. The menu planners were unhappy with us and our interference with their plans. They felt we had given them the reins and then taken them back.

There were other problems as well. Some parents did not understand this model and didn't see the value in self-directed study. Additionally, we didn't always know what each of us on the team was doing and which students were getting assistance and which were falling through the cracks.

TOUGH QUESTION:

? *How will you respond to a parent who says, "The middle school is not getting the students ready for high school"?*

Reflections

The next time we would like to have students not working all the time with their project-mates, but to form other groups with students working on different projects. This would allow students to share ideas, problem solve, and brainstorm with—and offer suggestions to—students from other groups. The students could then take back some ideas to their project team.

The biggest change we would make, though, has to do with communication. First, we would communicate more about the model with parents; second, we would make changes in team communication. We could carry around clipboards with a student roster. As we speak with students, we could keep a log for reference at team meetings. We could then decide who would meet with students with whom he had not interacted. This communication and coordination is essential. Without this, constructivist, active learning approaches may become disjointed, the curriculum pieces may no longer complement each other, and some students may feel lost.

TOUGH QUESTIONS:

?

- *How do you respond to a parent who comes to you with a statement such as: "My daughter has learned to think and that is good, but sometimes it makes her ask questions she shouldn't, like: 'Why should I have to study this?'"*
- *What is your vision about learning at a middle school?*

The High School: Student Boredom, Alienation, and the "Who Am I?" Question (Grades 9–12)

There are three main issues at the high school level. The first issue involves the "Who am I?" question. There are some high school students—particularly those whose confidence and identity are connected to high grades—who feel comfortable in the traditional system. They have mastered the schooling game, know how to memorize and recite back, know what the teacher wants, and feel safe. There are millions of other teenagers, however, who are bored, disinterested, and disconnected. It would be a rare teenager who woke up shouting to the rooftops: "I can't wait to get to math class and do calculus!" or "I can't wait to get to Mr. Gotha's class so we can watch a video of the New Deal," or "I can't wait to get to English today so I can practice grammar rules—AGAIN!" Typical adolescent lethargy is not only a result of boring teaching approaches but also a result of educators paying little attention to the developmental needs of their students. As with the emerging adolescents of the middle grades, high school students have priorities that often are unrelated to school (at least in traditional settings). Like middle schoolers, most are still asking, "Who am I?" In the traditional educational format, there is very little connection to this central question of identity.

From Adam to the Atom in 10 Months: Welcome to World History With Mr. Shoate

A second crucial issue at the high school level is that the curriculum is usually content driven. The problem here, as we discussed in Chapter 5, is that you can't separate curriculum from instructional approach, and if the high school curriculum is heavily weighted with lists of topics to be covered (as we suggest in the heading above), there is only one way for teachers to feel as if they are accomplishing what they are expected to do, and that is to disseminate information most of the time. This is especially true if teachers are still working in the traditional 40 or 50 minute time periods. Under pressure to get to World War I by the end of the year or to get to equations by January, teachers will deliver information as fast as they can and then move to the next topic. This approach does not allow for in-depth study or for ways for students to see connections among topics or disciplines or to see relevancy to their own lives.

TOUGH QUESTION:

> **?** *How could you convince teachers at your high school that students would not be hurt by learning in a different way and perhaps not **covering** as much content, but knowing and understanding more of what they did learn?*

Preparing for SATs and Other College Entrance Exams

A third issue you will ignore only at great peril is that of high school student preparation for the SAT and other college entrance exams. Whether they ought to be or not, these exams are a major concern for parents and teachers at the high school level. New teaching approaches are especially problematic for parents and administrators who ask: "Can active learning approaches, which focus on inquiry and depth of understanding rather than massive amounts of information, prepare students adequately for these exams?" Although there is much research showing that constructivist approaches lead to equal if not greater success in all academic areas (see Chapter 3), it is difficult to appease and convince parents and others with these reports. There are parents and students who will feel that time is being wasted, that the teachers are getting paid to teach (translate as "tell") and should be doing it, and that projects and activities may be entertaining but are essentially without substance and pointless. Even though we know (Clinchy, 1994; Conley, 1996; DiGiulio, 2004) that standardized tests for the most part do not measure the depth of, or ability to apply, understanding; and even though we know that more and more colleges are eliminating or making an option of the SATs; and even though we know that these kinds of test scores are not the best predictors of success in either college or life, if you are trying to make changes in your classroom, you have to be aware of these parental and administrator worries and issues, and you need to address them head on.

TOUGH QUESTION:

> **?** *How can high school teachers work with college professors to reduce the need high school teachers feel to cover material?*

Changing Times at Ridgemont High

In the Block

In our first edition of this book, we described the move in high schools toward block scheduling. At that time we wrote: "If you are a high school teacher who has not yet experienced block scheduling, you probably won't have to wait much longer. This change is happening everywhere—in some places through the actions of the administrators or teachers themselves and in other places through statewide efforts in educational reform. The rate of change to block scheduling in high schools is dramatic. Recent estimates are that at least 50% of American high schools have already changed, are currently studying how to change, or are in the process of changing to block scheduling" (Canady & Rettig, 1996).

As with recent changes at the middle school, since the advent of standardized testing and high school graduation testing requirements, some of this movement has slowed. However, anyone teaching at the high school should know about block scheduling and why it is supportive of a constructivist approach.

Why Block Scheduling?

It has long been known that 40- or 50-minute periods lead to fragmentation of learning. Think about this: Carlos is 15 years old in a traditional high school. He starts his first class at Pueblo High School at 7:45 a.m. In 40 minutes, the bell rings, and he switches gears not only in academic subjects but in classroom settings, processes, requirements, and dynamics for another 40 minutes. He does this seven or eight times a day. When he returns to the math class on the following day, after six or seven other 40-minute classes have disrupted that learning experience, he is expected to pick up where that class left off the day before. It is a disconnected, choppy curriculum at best with few, if any, connections among subject areas made apparent to the students.

Block scheduling allows teachers to have, for example, 90 minutes to conduct learning experiences connected to material formerly addressed in a 40-minute period. This extra time will allow students to become actively engaged in more in-depth learning and comprehension. Unfortunately, many teachers do not know how to handle block scheduling and don't know why it is happening. Some just continue to use traditional approaches and move into the 90-minute period what they formerly did in two 40-minute periods. Not only is this not the purpose of block scheduling, it won't work—how many teenagers do you know who can remain alert for a 90-minute lecture?

Moving In and Around the Block

For experienced teachers used to traditional scheduling, this change can be very unnerving. It is only natural that an extended period would seem to be just more of the same, only more difficult. It should be neither. It should generate very different kinds of learning approaches. It is not only the teachers who have to get used to something new. You can't expect students to jump into a new environment or system without warning or gradual change. In particular, you cannot expect them to do this if the assessment process changes as well and moves from a recite-it-back mode to a demonstration of understanding format. This can be most unnerving to the "A" students who have spent a school lifetime mastering that traditional system and who suddenly feel as if they will lose their edge when other students, who are more willing to take risks (after all their grades may already have been mostly mediocre), begin to shine. (See next part of this chapter for more on this issue.)

Addressing It All

This is a lot to think about: adolescent boredom, the adolescents' quest to find their identities, pressure from jam-packed curricula, students who will resist changes, students who demand change, parents and administrators who are worried about standardized testing, students and parents who are worried about graduation tests, and implications of block scheduling and interdisciplinary teaming for working conditions and professional relationships. As you introduce constructivist approaches, you need to be aware of and address these issues while keeping in mind that your main concern has to be student learning. As you read the following report of Katy Smith, see if you can determine how she addresses and has addressed these issues.

Meet Katy Smith

Katy Smith is an English teacher at Addison Trail High School in Addison, Illinois. Her descriptions and dialogue bring together the issues, questions, concerns, and possibilities of constructivist approaches—at the high school level in particular and at all grade levels in general.

The Process for Katy Smith and Her Teaching Partners Ralph Feese and Rob Hartwig: Students Negotiate the Curriculum

Katy and Ralph, English and social studies teachers respectively, first teamed to teach an 11th-grade American Studies Program that focused on history and literature, during the 1988–1989 school year. In the fifth year of this program, students became actively engaged in developing the curriculum. As with Ann and Janette at the middle grades, Katy and Ralph asked students to brainstorm questions they felt needed to be answered about a particular topic and then asked them to suggest, select, and follow through on activities that would help them answer the questions. Katy and Ralph gave few traditional tests during the semester, and what tests they did give were interdisciplinary, not separate history or English tests. They assessed students mainly through their papers, projects, and presentations (Smith, 1993). The details of this project's procedures are much the same as Ann and Janette describe in the previous section (see Beane, 1993, and Brodhagen et al., 1992), so we won't elaborate on them here. Instead, we will listen to Katy reflecting on the last several years of working with the American Studies Program as well as with the Freshmen Studies Program that she and Ralph subsequently piloted with science teacher Rob Hartwig.

Reflections

The Process/Content Issue

There is no such thing as learning a process unless you're learning that process doing something with meaningful content. We've really struggled over the past few years to define that particular issue. It is essential that kids be involved in the processes that involve thinking, but you can't learn to think without having something to think about. You've got to have the content there. As part of an interdisciplinary situation, I've been forced and challenged to examine what is the really essential, really important content. I get a little nervous about people who talk about covering the content because to cover is to obscure. There has to be a balance. The critical question to ask yourself is why a particular topic is important.

Interdisciplinary Curriculum

In interdisciplinary contexts students can get to look at a problem through different lenses. Let me give you an example from our class that we teach together. This is called Freshmen Studies and includes English, social studies, and now science since Rob has joined our team. One of the projects in which we have been involved is the Illinois Rivers Project. Basically what we have done is adopt a portion of Salt Creek that is a part of the Illinois River system. It's right in our community and takes us about five minutes by bus. Since we are teaming we have the first three periods of the day to schedule as a block.

The first time we took a trip out to the creek to plan what we wanted to do, we each found an angle that worked for us. Rob was really involved in water testing—getting the kids to take the samples to find out really specific bio-chemical kinds of things. Ralph had been doing some things with geographical features and talking about how meandering happens, how cut banks happen, how humans interact with the river. I had been looking at the river in terms of its symbolism and its power in literature and in music and how the experience of being on the river can inspire poetry and fiction.

Three Perspectives

Ralph had planned to do a geographical survey—to walk the kids up and down the creek and to have them look at the different elements—upstream, down stream, etc. Rob was going to do water testing, and I thought of sitting and looking at the relationship between nature and humans and the environment and different points of view—in the creek, on the side of the creek. We got on the buses to go back to school and each of us looked like the cat who had swallowed the canary because each of us had gotten to do the things which dealt with important concepts connected to our three disciplines and which we really enjoyed. But for the kids, it was an experience from three different perspectives. Some liked certain parts better than others, but everyone liked some part of the experience, and their follow-up work demonstrated a high level of learning. Some kids got into writing letters to the water commission and the forest preserve district. Others said things like, "I never knew that forest preserve was there— that's a really great place to go."

Subsequent Trips to the River

A couple of times since then, we have had our math teacher join us. Math is not part of our block schedule at this time because the students are at such different levels of readiness, and we haven't been able to figure out how to incorporate math on a full-time basis. But the math department chairperson came out to the creek with us and he did some things with the kids about how to measure the depth, how to determine the flow of the creek, and then he gave them a problem: If you knew the rate at which the creek was flowing, if the gymnasium was this big, how long would it take for the creek to fill up the gym? Again, kids said things like, "I hadn't ever considered any of these things. I hadn't ever looked at it in this way."

Becoming Your Own PR Person: Addressing Concerns

SATs and College Preparation

We have been very aware of the concerns of parents and administrators in regard to student preparation for college in relation to our interdisciplinary and student-developed curriculum. We have been conducting follow-up studies to address this kind of concern, So far in the data, there is nothing to indicate that kids are not making appropriate academic progress. Illinois has a set of assessments that kids have to take at various points. The data our assessment center has gathered shows that the students in our program are doing as well as or slightly better than their peers. They certainly aren't going down. What we hear from teachers, for better or worse, is that these student have good questioning skills and know how to generate and identify problems and propose possible solutions. For example, at a recent in-service meeting, one of our social studies colleagues recently commented that he can tell in his classes which of the students who are now juniors and seniors came from our Freshmen Studies program because when it comes time to do library research, they are the ones to say, "Oh, OK" and off they go, whereas kids who were not in the program have more trouble and need a lot of direction.

Getting Parents and Administrators on Board

You have to get parents and administrators involved if you want their support. One of the things we do at the end of each quarter is to have our students lead conferences with their parents. The first conference, we invite the parents in; second quarter they do it at home because it's around the holidays; for the third quarter we offer an option—traditional teacher/parent conference or a conference between parent and student; and then fourth quarter we have a big culminating project to which we invite the parents.

The most powerful thing about student-led conferences is that kids are responsible for sharing their portfolios and daily binders—the portfolios are best works portfolios and the binders show what the students have done daily—and the kids have to explain what is happening in my classroom. The students have to schedule the appointments and send invitations—some kids prefer to have the conference with another teacher, a coach, or a guidance person (not all parents can be there). We hear a lot from the parents: "OK, we finally understand this." So, one of the ways we get support is to do a lot of inviting—please come into my classroom, please feel free—it gets exhausting, but the benefits are worth it. We also invite other teachers and the administration and guidance in when students have exhibitions.

Planning Time

Any time teachers are going to work together, it's important to have planning time and to meet in places where others can see you are meeting. We really pushed administration a number of years ago until all of us who taught American Studies at the time had a common planning period. We would get together on Wednesdays, third period, and go down to the back of the cafeteria and have our meeting there. This was fairly deliberate and it's worthwhile. If you meet in a place where people can see you are actually using this time—that the schedule hassle is worth it—you will get support. You need to invite people in.

Breathing Deeply and Diving In

When people ask me how to get started in making the shift from a teacher centered, top-down classroom situation to a situation where emphasis is on student learning, I often refer them to Nancie Atwell's book In the Middle *(1987). Somewhere in there she makes a statement to the effect that if you are not sure how to begin, just take a deep breath and begin. Start somewhere and try something—try a project where you turn the responsibility over to the students. Yes, everyone has mandated curriculum and we are the specialists. Were supposed to know what is important, but often we don't give the kids enough credit for what they already know or credit for their ability to ask good questions.*

Making the Mind Shift

This is the most difficult part. When kids come and say, "I don't have the research done," or "I don't have the book," it is so easy to fall into the trap of responding, "Well let me write you a pass," or even, "That's tough, you can't go to your locker." Another way to respond is: "Well that's a problem. How can you solve it?" Put it right back on them. A young lady said to me a couple of weeks ago, "Well my partner isn't here so I can't do anything," and I said, "What do you mean? You have the capability to work on these problems yourself—on your proposal." She replied, "Well, I think that's stupid. I said, "I'm sorry you feel that way however if you don't work on this, what else could you be doing?"

Practicing What You Will Say

Start by thinking, "What am I going to say when the student says, 'I don't want to'?" Don't get into a power struggle. This isn't a power issue. The students have to be empowered. They are the ones who will or will not learn. "Gee, that's a problem, how do you intend to solve it?" Practice this speech. It's hard to let go. It's particularly hard if you have a flop early on. One of the advantages of being on a team is that you know it's not only you. Somebody is there to support you when things don't go well, and there's someone to celebrate with you when they do go well.

The hardest thing for me to deal with was a colleague who said I was abdicating my response as a teacher—that I was being irresponsible in allowing the kids to have so much say in the classroom. That was the toughest confrontation I've ever had, and we're still at an impasse. It is a common misconception that if you have students developing curriculum, students do whatever they want. Constructivist approaches do not mean that. Because students have a choice in a writer's workshop doesn't mean there is no rigor, that the students are doing inappropriate things. This is the real hard one, I have prepared answers for these kinds of questions and at this point I ask if they want to see the contracts my students and I have. Invite people in—let them see what is going on.

PRESERVICE AND NOVICE TEACHERS:

How will you respond to a colleague who calls you irresponsible for using constructivist approaches?

Demonstrating

Sometimes you need to do what we call a little "creative insubordination" to do something risky. In other words, just close the door and try it. If it works, share it. Show it to everyone. You have to have confidence in yourself. We want to try but you don't have to make it public up front. Success breeds success. The more others see that what is happening is quite extraordinary in terms of student learning, the more they will support you and will want to try it themselves.

Successes

Not everything has worked the way we wish it would have, but I stand by what I wrote a few years ago. That is:

Once we began negotiating curriculum with our students, we noticed the conspicuous absence of stereotypical classroom habits. . . . Through the hardships of creating our classes, we experienced democracy in all its complexity. Through negotiating curriculum the students came to accept more responsibility for their learning. For Ralph and me [and now Rob], the process has affirmed the validity of our basic beliefs about our students. The students have shown us that they really can solve problems—if we just let them. (Smith, 1993, p. 37)

Constructivist Teachers
Meet the Mandates Head On

In the next part of this chapter, we meet three teachers who have developed and sustained constructivist classrooms and approaches in spite of the pressures of the mandated standards, testing, and the No Child Left Behind (NCLB) Act. Each of the experiences is different and walks us through various kinds of successes and issues related to implementing constructivist approaches. (Names are pseudonyms; people and events are real.)

Don Mahony and Unexpected Parental Reaction

Don, a math and science teacher in a rural Vermont middle school, in an attempt to make his classroom more constructivist, abandoned the typical and traditional math program and replaced it with more progressive and active learning environments that allowed students to develop and solve mathematical problems relating to, and through the process of, the building of structures. In the process, students ages 9–10 were involved in complex mathematical calculations including algebraic and geometric functions advanced far beyond their grade and age level. This did not surprise Don. What did blindside him were the hostile, angry, frightening, and sometimes threatening responses from some of the parents of those students who had until this point in their schooling been the stars of academia. The parents were furious that "those other" students (those who had previously been the poor performers or nonachievers) were succeeding in ways that their children were not.

TOUGH QUESTIONS:

?
- *What do issues of power and stakeholding (for example, for the parents of traditionally high succeeding students) have to do with this kind of unexpected and frightening parental responses?*
- *What measures would you take to avoid the problem of students who succeed in traditional settings but not as well in constructivist settings (and their parents) becoming hostile and fearful as the processes and expectations change in the classroom?*

What Are Your Fears?

We have seen in Chapter 3 how entrenched traditional processes are. Is this resistance to change the result of teachers' lack of understanding of progressive, active approaches? Is it the result of teachers blindly following mandates? Is it the result of teachers' fears of losing a job if their students don't perform as required by the State on the standardized tests? Is it the result of fear on the part of the power stakeholders (including top achieving students, their parents, their teachers, and administrators), as in Don's experience, that if students in other than the top academic levels succeed, these stakeholders will lose power and status?

To give context to these issues and to generate further questions, here we present three case studies of constructivist approaches and how students in these programs moved from positions of low achievement and/or alienation in traditional educational classrooms to become engaged high achievers.

Marie Hall and Ann and the MA Advisory

Marie Hall, the Teacher

Marie was a faculty member for three years at the progressive, public, and voluntary Metropolitan Regional Career and Technical Center (MET) School in Rhode Island. At the MET, students create internships for themselves that allow them to problem solve in an area of personal interest (Levine, Sizer, & Washor, 2001) and simultaneously meet appropriate learning standards. Two years ago, Ms. Hall left the MET to develop a MET-like alternative program, the MA (Morris Academy) Advisory, in a rural public high school in north-central Vermont.

Ann, the Student

Ann came to the MA Advisory at the beginning of her sophomore year. Marie reports:

> *Until she joined the Advisory, Ann's self-image was mediocre at best . . .*

> **"I felt [in freshman year] like I could never keep up no matter how hard I tried. The only thing I liked about school was my art class and seeing my friends at lunch. . . . I got homework from every class, and it was so hard to keep track of it, hard to get it all done. . . . It was overwhelming when I would see a huge book or reading assignment or a big packet of worksheets for science or have to take a test. I didn't know where to start. I thought I would grow up and work at the mountain [ski resort] like my mom."**

> *When Ann reflects on the Advisory, though, her view is very different:*

> **"When I first joined, I didn't know what to think. . . . The good thing about the advisory is that we have to focus on just a few things that we're really interested in rather than a whole bunch of things that aren't connected. It is much less confusing, and this way I really learn things—not just memorize them and then forget them. I've learned that most of the things I'm interested in have to do with science. I want to understand all kinds of things about the human body—how eyes work and why some people need glasses, the structure of teeth, and cancer, especially leukemia. . . . I even want to take the biology class next year."**

Results

> *By the end of her freshman year in the traditional classroom, Ann had earned only 28 out of 35 required credits and had a cumulative GPA for the year of 79.4% (70% is passing). Her grades ranged from a 95% in music and acting to a failing 60% in science. After her first semester in the Advisory, Ann's cumulative GPA for the year was at 91.9%, and she had earned 20.5 credits–almost as many in one semester as she earned all of last year.*

> **"Before, I never wanted to go to college. . . . Now I know that I can do it—I might need to look for a college with certain kinds of help, but I really want to do something in science or in the medical field, so I know I have to go."**

TOUGH QUESTIONS:

?
- *After the successes of the Advisory's first year, parents representing higher socioeconomic levels than students already in the program suddenly wanted their children in the program. Why do you think this happened?*

- *If, unlike the students in these narratives, "lower" achieving students did not succeed in progressive educational programs, but "higher" achievers did, would progressive education become the norm? Why? Why not?*

Matt Manino and Michael and a Multi-Age, Integrated, Thematic Classroom

Matt Manino, the Teacher

Matt taught grades 5–8 in a rural K–8 school in northwestern Vermont for several years. Matt developed and conducted his classes in a progressive and constructivist environment that required the students to initiate, investigate, problem-solve, and discover.

Michael, the Student

Matt reports:

Michael started his fifth-grade year as a disenfranchised, at-risk student. His mother had recently died of cancer, his father was an alcoholic, and his older brother was in prison. Michael lived in a three-room camp with no electricity. At school he demonstrated little self-determination or self-efficacy. In his traditional elementary classroom, he refused to participate in many activities that involved reading and math. Michael spent extended periods of time in the principal's office for discipline purposes. He was failing all of his classes, he received no support at home, and many of the school and community members determined that he was destined to follow in his brother's path.

Michael in a Constructivist Setting

The following year Michael was moved to my multi-age classroom where I taught language arts, science, and social studies using a theme based, integrated curriculum model that used a three-hour block schedule each morning. Michael's math teacher continued to teach math each afternoon using a traditional curriculum and approach. In my integrated classroom, Michael learned the skills to educate himself and identified his personal learning style. He learned how to ask critical questions, set goals, make connections to prior knowledge and demonstrate mastery of concepts using multiple modalities. He practiced strategies which I modeled for understanding new information.

Results

Michael was able to accept responsibility for learning and was able successfully to investigate topics of personal interest in relation to specific state standards. To meet

the standard of explaining the forces that shape the earth, for example, Michael gen-
erated a list of questions relating to a nearby eroded stream. He then researched his
questions, built a model of the stream to demonstrate how wind and water caused the
erosion, and taught a group of his peers about what he had learned.

Over the three years in my class, Michael transformed from a passive protagonist
to an actively engaged member of a learning community. His behavior problems dimin-
ished, and he willingly took on a leadership role in the class, often volunteering to help
new students learn the skills he had mastered. Sadly, the energetic, outgoing student in
this class returned to noncompliance during the rigid traditional math class.

TOUGH QUESTIONS:

?
- What attributes, dispositions, and talents are required of students to succeed in traditional classrooms?

- What attributes, dispositions, and talents are required of students to succeed in progressive and student-centered classrooms?

Don Mahony and the Freshman Class and Standardized Testing

Don Mahony, the Teacher

A year ago, Don moved from the middle school as described above and started his first year as a math teacher at a rural, traditional high school in northeastern Vermont after teaching middle school math and science for several years.

Don continues his determination to create constructivist classrooms and experiences. Don reports:

At the beginning of the 2003 school year, 140 out of 250 incoming freshmen at this underachieving, state-targeted high school [where Don was teaching] tested well below an eighth-grade level in math. To respond, the math department developed a Fundamentals of Math course (against the directives of the State consultants who came to the school to "save the day") which focused on problem solving and compu-tation without calculators. The state consultants and an additional state specialist assigned to "save" this school informed the math department that the Fundamentals course would not work and that the students would be deficit in computation forever. The math department ignored the state consultants.

Results

By the end of the first semester, the students in the Fundamentals course had com-pleted a year of math and retook the diagnostic test. Of the 140 students, 97 placed in the ninth-grade level and passed on to either Algebra 1 or the constructivist, conceptual, and integrated Interactive Mathematics Program (IMP) (Fendel, Resek, Alper, & Fraser, 1997). The students who graduated out of the Fundamentals course and are now in IMP are demonstrating greater confidence and ability in math than are the "smart" students who are now in precalculus. Their work ethic has become strong. More importantly, the National Standard Reference Exam (NSRE) scores are beginning to show that the students in the problem-solving and integrated constructivist IMP program are outperforming the students in the traditional math classes.

TOUGH QUESTIONS:

?
- *Why do the typically higher-achieving students in traditional classrooms often resist progressive approaches while the lower-achieving students rarely do?*
- *These narratives describe students who were not succeeding in traditional classrooms. What about students who succeed in traditional classrooms but falter to a demonstrable degree in progressive classrooms? Why does this happen and who are the power stakeholders in this scenario?*

Moving On

It is almost time to *Dive In* with projects similar to what teachers describe in this chapter or to at least *Get Your Feet Wet* with the models and processes in Chapter 6. Before you do, there are three more stops you ought to make on this journey. It would be omitting a major chunk of what is happening in classrooms today if we neglected to talk about technology in relation to constructivist approaches. This we do in the next chapter. It would be even more remiss to try to implement constructivist models without discussing the implications of diversity in our classrooms. Chapters 9 and 10 raise important issues about, and provide recommendations for, dealing with diversity.

Before you move on—three more serious challenges:

THREE CHALLENGES:

How would you develop a teacher preparation program that would prepare teachers to think and speak critically in relation to top-down mandates?

Develop a theory that could explain how issues of societal power are connected to the propositions, assumptions, and mandates such as the NCLB Act.

Define the role of a teacher in a democracy.

Technology: Untangling the Web

8

It is almost impossible to keep up with what is happening in the world of technology. In our first edition we reported:

Although the amount and kinds of technology schools have differ widely, during the 1996–1997 academic year many schools were in a mad rush to get wired; that is, to get networked in the computer lab, networked throughout the school, and networked to cyberspace. A report (1995) from the U.S. Office of Technology Assessment (OTA) estimated that there had been an increase of about 700,000 computers in schools for each of the last 3 years, that about 35% of schools had some kind of computer network, and that almost all schools had TVs and VCRs (O'Neil, 1995).

Here are some of the things that have happened in the last eight years in terms of the wiring of schools and providing computers:

- Nearly every school in the United States has access to computers and the Internet.
- Most schools have computers and the Internet access in classrooms.
- The majority of schools have the most recent operating software for their computers.
- Estimates are that there are 4.1 computers per student.
- In the state of Maine, every teacher and student in grades 7 and 8 are provided with laptops and handheld devices.
- Virtual schools allow students to take courses on-line in 21 states (Park & Staresina, 2004).

Unfortunately, the same problem exists now as did then: Teachers do not have expertise in integrating technology into the learning experiences for the purpose of enhancing student learning. In the 2003 NAEP (National Assessment of Educational Progress), it is reported that with regard to math teachers of fourth graders, the overwhelming majority used computers for drill and practice or math games. Very few were using computers for higher-order thinking tasks (Park & Staresina, 2004).

Cuban (2001) examined public schools and college classes in Silicon Valley, figuring that if technology use was noteworthy anywhere it would be there in the center of technological innovation. He was trying to determine if the availability of computers had changed or was changing approaches to teaching and learning. Although he found some creative pockets, overall he found that the use of computers was limited and that the use had had little effect on traditional classroom practice or learning. He argues that fewer than 10% of teachers use computers seriously and what use there is, is sporadic and uncreative.

Like the teachers in Cuban's study, you may be feeling overwhelmed and pressured trying to figure out what this equipment all means, how it all works, and what to do with it all. Have you also asked yourself: How does (or can) any of this enhance learning, and why should I use any of it? How is any of it connected to a constructivist learning experience?

TOUGH QUESTIONS:

> **?** How can teacher education programs prepare students to be teachers who know how and when to use technology in constructivist classrooms? How will teacher preparation programs have to change to accomplish this?

Where Are We Going With Technology in Constructivist Classrooms?

In 1913, Thomas Edison optimistically predicted that books would soon be obsolete, that it would be possible to teach every branch of human knowledge with the motion picture, and that school systems would be completely changed in 10 years (Saettler, 1968). In the 1960s, Skinner believed his teaching machine would revolutionize education. Seymour Papert (1980), developer of LOGO, assured us in the early 1980s that a radical change in education was possible and that change was directly tied to computers—that there would be as much technology in schools as there were pens and pencils. In the late 1980s, Mary Alice White, director of the Electronic Learning Laboratory at Teachers College, Columbia University, contended that technology would alter learning and learning environments, change content, and "enable almost anyone to learn almost anything" (in Levin, 1987, p. 6). In the early 1990s, it was the Apple Schools of Tomorrow, and now we have all kinds of networked multimedia systems, interactive whiteboards, hand-held devices, a multitude of new kinds of technology products, and the World Wide Web.

According to Clifford Stoll (in O'Neil, 1996), however, schools buy and promote technology (usually translated as "computers") with little thought about the educational process. Can technology enhance student learning? Have the schools been duped by media hype and high-powered salespeople? The U.S. government may think so. It has switched its emphasis (Education Week, 2004) from wiring schools to determining whether or not the investment has been worth it in terms of student learning and achievement (Education Week, 2004).

TOUGH QUESTION:

> **?** As a teacher how do you get over your anxiety connected to using technology?

If you use technology to do the same things you were doing in a traditional format, we would have to ask: Why bother? If, on the other hand, technology can help to develop or to complement and extend constructivist ideas and approaches, then it can be very valuable. The same propositions we have used to define constructivist class-rooms thus far are the same propositions you need to use when determining if your use of technology advances or hinders constructivist goals. Are students discovering for themselves? Are they developing problems and questions, investigating and searching for data, and finding resolutions? Are they interpreting and synthesizing materials that they find? Are they using the technology to become independent and empowered thinkers who do not depend on the opinions of others? Are students developing new knowledge or simply shuffling information around?

You, Your School, and Technology

What is happening at your school with technology? Has the school just purchased and networked computers? Are you wondering how to use them? What technology do you have available? Do you have an interactive whiteboard in your room? Do you have a tablet you can use from anywhere in the room to work the whiteboard? How *can* a teacher integrate technology effectively and effortlessly to create active learning processes?

Avoiding the DVD Trap

Have you ever watched what happens when a teacher tells a class they are going to view a DVD, videotape, or a TV show? Usually, the students tune out, catch up on lost sleep, or, if they are teenagers, pass notes around about the Saturday night party. Regardless of the time spent in preparation for the presentation or use of these tech-nologies, unless the teacher has found an extraordinary prepackaged program, which most are not, he or she will lose the students. If you've ever used these programs your-self, you know that even you might be napping, correcting papers, or daydreaming.

What do you see when students are using computers? What we have seen and see often are: (1) students typing reports that consist merely of words and phrases taken from the Web; or (2) students spending a whole class period trying to draw the funni-est nose for a science report about smell; or (3) a student dragging clip art around and making "click here" buttons so other students can look at various pieces of this art. The students then connect what they have found to a few sentences and call it a report. This is not active learning. Clearly, just using lots of technology does not guarantee that you are using constructivist approaches. Students need to be actively involved in their own learning. As long as they are passive, as with the "sit and watch" or with the "sit, input, watch, move objects and text around, then sit, input, and move objects and text around some more" use of educational media, they will suffer terminal (sorry, no pun intended) boredom. As Rousseau might say, they will become stupid and passive. In any event, they will learn little.

What Is Technology Anyway?

It is a mistaken idea that computers represent the only educational technology available. If you are in a school that has few computers, you don't have to panic.

There are many kinds of technology you can use to complement and create constructivist classrooms. Let's look at some of the technology you probably already use or have used and see how you might use it to advance constructivist goals.

The Overhead Projector

It's difficult to imagine a school without an overhead projector. If you use the overhead projector to show notes or diagrams to the students, that is a traditional format. As helpful and as necessary as this may be in your classes at various times and for various purposes, there are other, more productive ways to use the overhead. For example, in any of the models referred to in Chapter 6, once students have decided on an investigation or activity, they need to find, interpret, and synthesize their material and demonstrate understanding. Students can show that they have analyzed and that they understand material or have solved problems by using overheads and a tape recorder. They can create the overheads by drawing visuals such as diagrams, charts, or figures that would clearly indicate analysis and comprehension of the topic; they can then write a complementary script and record this on an audiotape that will accompany the overhead visuals. This tape can either introduce provocative questions relating to the drawings or create related problems for the whole class to solve. This changes the activity from a deadly *presentation* to an interactive learning experience.

A group of fifth graders from an inner-city Indianapolis school that had almost no technology equipment (and a very, very old overhead projector) created a similar demonstration for their project in National History Day a few years ago and blew the judges (professional historians) away with their in-depth analysis. The point is that you don't need complicated technology to allow students to be creative, to demonstrate understanding, and to conduct investigations. You don't need complicated technology to enhance learning.

PowerPoint Shows

Even some kindergarten children know how to create a PowerPoint show. If you haven't tapped into this remarkable program and capability, make an effort to get your school system to provide a workshop on the how-tos and the limitless possibilities of PowerPoint. The danger here is that most of the workshops with which we are familiar do nothing other than perpetuate the traditional approach to teaching and learning. The PowerPoint show becomes the presentation in place of the teacher's lecture. Sometimes a better way to learn how to work a program is to ask the students to teach you. There is always someone who knows how to do it.

What students have to do to make this constructivist is to create PowerPoint shows that demonstrate they understand concepts related to particular standards, but *at the same time involve the whole class in active learning or problem solving.* How do they do that? And what ages can handle that? Well, most **teachers can't** handle it; however, in grades as early as the second, we have seen students doing just as we describe with an excitement and ability that is amazing. Here you have an opportunity to ask the students how they could do this. Get them to brainstorm ideas. You might be shell-shocked with the possibilities they define.

As part of the process of investigating and figuring out, students can create a script to accompany the PowerPoint show. They can add appropriate music that adds to the demonstration of understanding or enhances the issues for other students. Finally, they can engage class members by asking them to analyze slides in various ways.

This process can be as simple as a student manually running the PowerPoint slide show while discussing the issues and concepts or as complicated as one or more students preparing an audiotape of their narration, then letting the program drive the slide show automatically. What goes into creating the slide show—doing library research, interviewing (by phone or in person) famous and not-so-famous people, reviewing primary sources, taking live and book photos, analyzing the material, writing a script, and merging it all into an understandable and provocative production—is what makes this exercise constructivist. National History Day at the University of Maryland also can provide examples of these shows for you (see http://nationalhisto ryday.org).

Documentary Video/CD Making

Many students now have video cameras, and many schools have at least one camera that students can use. Some schools have editing equipment and others have the local cable station housed in their building. Cable stations allow students to do more sophisticated technical work and often allow them to broadcast their video throughout the school network. Although students have to learn how to use the camera and the editing equipment, it is once again the research and investigation, the interviewing, the analysis, and the synthesis into a final product that is constructivist.

DID YOU KNOW?

Were you aware that cable stations are required by Federal law to provide, free of charge, equipment and instruction on that equipment. You can contact your local cable station and inform them you have students who want or need to learn how to operate the technology and how to edit. Set up a time to make this happen.

If students fall asleep when watching DVDs, videos, and TV programs, why won't they fall asleep when student productions are used? There is research (Page, 1992) to indicate that the opposite occurs when students develop the media productions. Students in the audience become actively involved and curious about these peer productions and messages. Remember Marshall McLuhan and Quentin Fiore's (1967) *The Medium Is the Massage*? When student productions are the medium, it makes a difference for the audience. Why would this be?

Here is what some student participants in National History Day thought about this issue:

Jim thought students were actively engaged when watching other students' media productions because the students wanted to evaluate their own documentaries in relation to some other student's. Ed and Amosh, however, argued that it had more to do with knowing how difficult developing a media presentation was and in having empathy for the student producer. Amosh also argued that adolescents were more trusting of other adolescents and would put more stock in a student's production than in a professionally developed one because "they're [professionals] paid to do that and you kind of get this negative thing in your mind." (Page, 1992, p. 328)

Computers

Stories abound in the literature about futuristic uses of computers in schools. For one example, look at the first edition of *Creating and Sustaining the Constructivist Classroom* and revisit the story of Chatham Lake School. This provides one example of how computers and technology can alter the entire organizational system of schooling as well as the nature of the learning experience. We recognize, however, that some schools don't have as many computers per student as other schools. For those of you working in such schools, we have included in this section some ways that you can use computers in existing traditional school systems and still have constructivist learning experiences.

Computers and Software

We'll start with the simplest use of computers. Some software currently on the market can facilitate constructivist learning experiences; other software is dreadful and does nothing but reinforce traditional methods or drill and repeat. Most educational programs developed for sale in retail stores are what we call *edutainment*. They are loaded with razzle dazzle that is simply irrelevant to the task. Sometimes the real task, if you look closely, is not what is advertised as educational but something else that is quite trivial. For example, a well-known program that claims to teach geography does not in fact demand any use of geography to complete the sequence of activities. The student is required only to do some rudimentary pattern matching of pictures. Although the student may pick up some geographical trivia, she is not likely to develop any deep understanding of the subject by playing the game.

True constructivist programs engage students in extended problem solving. The best software packages we have found belong to Tom Snyder Productions of Watertown, Massachusetts. Everything that company produces is focused on and grounded in constructivist propositions. Table 8.1 provides a short list of criteria that can be used to identify the essential philosophy of an educational software program. Some programs may have characteristics of more than one type, and some programs don't fit any category well.

Multimedia Systems

Some schools have multimedia computer systems that allow students to combine many technologies and materials in one place. This technology can include a digital still/video camera with which students can take moving or still pictures that are then fed right into the computer program or learning experience that the students are developing. Additionally, scanners can scan into the same document any pictures or

TABLE 8.1: Identifying the Philosophy of the Software Program			
Criteria for Classifying Software	Information Delivery (Transmission)	Edutainment	Constructivist
Way student spends time	Student is mostly absorbing rather than using information.	Student spends a lot of time passively watching the screen.	Student is active, engaged in problem solving. Software can often be used to create permanent products.
Who controls the sequence of activity	The computer	Usually the computer	The student
Way of confirming and acknowledging learning	The student passes tests or quizzes and is usually rewarded with audiovisual congratulations.	The student completes the sequence and is rewarded with audiovisual congratulations.	The student solves problems or produces a product that may be shown to and evaluated by other students, teachers, or members of the community.
Mental state after extended use	Student often becomes tried.	The students' eyes glaze over.	Student remains alert and engaged.

words the students have or that they create. To add to this, students can retrieve materials from the Web, from libraries, and from e-mail lists. There is also sound capability connected to these setups. If students use all this equipment to simply retrieve, input, and move information or visuals around, this is **not** constructivist. You want true investigating, figuring out, and problem solving related to content to occur. The final document should be the result of the student's analysis, interpretation, and synthesis of all gathered or produced material.

In addition, there are now wireless carts which hold laptops that can be distributed to students so that they can work at their tables or desks either individually, in pairs or groups, or as part of a whole class networked system. The students can have wireless connections to the Internet. There are also *tablets* that look like small laptops and allow students to write (really write in script) and use functions similar to laptop computers.

One of the most useful and most exciting new pieces of equipment is the interactive whiteboard, which is connected to a computer. These come in moveable board sizes (they look like movie screens) and much more portable sizes that have big projection possibilities. These are truly interactive and allow students to use their fingers as the mouse on the board, create from the board, print to a printer, save to a computer, and in general liven up the room and learning activity. Students seem energized by the use and possibilities of these boards. Students learn to be active in front of a class, creative in terms of what they are projecting on the board, and inventive in terms of using the board's capabilities to involve the class in learning. These boards can connect to Internet sound, video, photos, material, text, etc. If this overwhelms you, turn it over to your technology-literate students and let them be the instructors in how to use the equipment. In a district near Philadelphia, all schools have interactive whiteboards in every classroom. But as Cuban found in Silicon Valley, many of the boards sit idle because the teachers have no idea what to do with them. Does the use of the boards enhance learning? It depends on how they are used. Does the use of the boards engage students? **Definitely.** Does engagement mean greater learning? Try it and find out. What is important is not what equipment you have but how you use it to make learning experiences active and student owned.

There Is No End to This Chapter

One chapter in a book that focuses on how to create constructivist classrooms cannot do justice to the issues, advances, possibilities, and questions connected to technology. Additionally, there is so much happening so quickly with regard to technology in schools that much of this chapter probably is outdated as we write. We also know we have left out important items here such as Web literacy instruction, distance learning, and two-way conferencing. What we have done is provide you with a beginning. It's your turn to make it happen. Get cracking.

A SUGGESTION:

There are several publications focusing specifically on technology use in a constructivist class. We would recommend the following:

Learning with Technology: A Constructivist Perspective by D. Jonassen, K. Peck, and B. Wilson. Published by Merrill in 1999.

Multiculturalism: Making the Most of the Classroom Mosaic

9

Recently, we visited a student teacher in a small elementary school in the northwestern corner of rural Vermont. Imagine our surprise to find a sign on the front door for parents, written in Vietnamese! Schools are changing, and they are changing fast. The arrival of new immigrant groups, the mainstreaming of children with disabilities, and the precipitous rise in poverty among children have all contributed to making our classrooms more diverse—and in more ways—than at any other time in our nation's history. In fact, children are the most diverse segment of American society. Although student diversity makes teaching more challenging, this is problematic only if the focus is on how the teacher will deliver instruction rather than on how the students will learn. Classroom settings with students from different cultures, abilities, needs, and interests provide rich learning opportunities, in part because they so clearly reflect one of the central tenets of constructivism: There is virtually an infinite variety of ways to know the world. The magnitude of student diversity underscores this point in ways impossible to ignore by even the most traditional of teachers.

How Are Our Schools Changing?

Consider the following compiled from the National Center for Education Statistics (2003):

- Close to 60% of the nation's entire immigrant population entered the United States in the 1980s. A century ago, the nations that sent the largest numbers of immigrants had a common European culture (England, Ireland, Germany, and Italy). The nations that send the most immigrants now come from every corner of the globe. In rank order, they are Mexico, the Philippines, Korea, China, Taiwan, India, Cuba, the Dominican Republic, Jamaica, Canada, Vietnam, the United Kingdom, and Iran.
- As a group, children are America's poorest citizens. During the 1980s, the poverty rate for children reached an unprecedented 11%; by 1993, the level had increased to 23% (or more than one in five school-aged children; Hodgkinson, 1993). Today, more than one-fifth of all children continue to live below the poverty line, and children under the age of six have the highest rates of poverty.

- The two largest minority groups, Hispanic Americans and African Americans, together compose about one-third of the total school enrollment; currently, non-European American students are the majority in the 25 largest school districts in the country.
- By 2020 demographers predict that students of color will compose about half of the nation's school children.
- In 15 years, predictions indicate that Hispanic students will comprise more than one-fifth of the school age population.
- More than 15% of students in the schools of New York, Chicago, Los Angeles, Washington, D.C., and San Francisco are of limited English proficiency.

In addition, the United States Bureau of the Census estimates that there are 329 languages other than English spoken in the United States.

Do These Differences Affect Learning?

Simply put, "Yes." There is overwhelming evidence that such factors as a student's country of origin, cultural heritage, linguistic background, and religious beliefs, as well as the socioeconomic status of the student's parents, all in their own way, influence learning. Teachers who fail to recognize how the values of traditional schooling may clash with particular cultural values (Kugelmass, 1995) often face classrooms of disengaged, unmotivated, and/or disruptive learners who may find school irrelevant, or even hostile, to their values.

The Problem

As suggested above, today's teachers are required to be sensitive to a wider range of multicultural differences than ever before. Most teachers in the United States are white. More than one-third of the school-aged population is nonwhite; minority students already are the majority culture in many large urban school districts. Although eager to learn, teachers as a group believe they are unprepared to teach students from diverse cultures (Barry & Lechner, 1995). Can teachers package content into a single format that all children can understand? Or should they continuously repackage the content for each of the cultural, religious, and ethnic groups represented in their classrooms?

Liberating Ourselves

Framing the issues in this way reveals the potency of teacher commitment to thinking about teaching as information dispensing. As Barry and Lechner (1995) report, teachers are concerned primarily with how they will relate content in multiple ways to meet the needs of a very diverse student body. It should come as no surprise that teachers feel that this is a daunting task for which they are ill prepared. In fact, this is not a daunting task at all; it is an impossible one. Although some find this enormously distressing, we believe it is very liberating; as teachers, we cannot simultaneously be all things to all children. Nor can we present one approach based on a kind of average of student difference. Rather, we must reframe our questions about teaching and learning. We must do so to allow for student exploration and inquiry in a way that allows them to connect content knowledge to what they already know. How is this possible for students with limited English proficiency? How can teachers meet the needs of Mexican-American children, children of Asian-Pacific descent, and African-American children, all of whom are in the same classroom?

Focusing on Students' Experiences

Ethnic differences are real, but continually seeking to alter our teaching style to conform to our beliefs about each student (based solely on his or her ethnic identity) perpetuates an overgeneralization about ethnic groups and puts the focus of the teaching and learning experience in the wrong place. Knowing that Asian children as a group are quieter and more submissive to authority will not enhance the learning of students of Asian descent if, as a teacher armed with this knowledge, you continue to focus on what you will do to *cover* the curriculum as opposed to focusing on the ways you can help your students connect content to the most important factors in student learning—the students' experiences and prior knowledge (Ausubel, 1968).

The value of constructivism is that it respects and allows each student to use his or her unique knowledge and experience in the learning process. This is so whether the student is from a 10,000-acre ranch in Billings, Montana, or a one-room flat in Springfield, Massachusetts.

Finding Social Capital in the Margins

Diversity makes teaching more challenging, but it also provides wonderful opportunities; opportunities that new teachers should not ignore in an attempt to satisfy homogenous, inflexible, standards-driven curriculum and instruction. Traditional and nativist educators look on our nation's growing diversity as, at best, troublesome, or, at worst, a societal challenge to be controlled, suppressed, ignored, or dismissed. In their view, schools should seek to assimilate students from other cultures in order to perpetuate a narrow view of what it means to be American and to live in a democracy. Multiculturalists, on the other hand, view the growing diversity of our citizenry as an opportunity for increased societal richness, participation, understanding, and strength.

The multicultural educator James A. Banks suggests that mainstream curriculum should be revised at the "social action" level to encourage in students greater critical thinking and deeper pluralistic perspectives (Banks, Cookson, & Hawley, 2001, p. 198). He points out that the most common approach to multiculturalism typically involves no more than a brief review of the contributions of a few minority personalities and an introduction to traditional festivals, a method often derisively referred to as the *heroes and holidays* approach.

TOUGH QUESTIONS:

?

- *How do race, ethnicity, language, and social class interact to influence the behavior of your students?*

- *How about your own behavior? Is teaching and learning more challenging when you and your students share few if any of these characteristics?*

New teachers must seek out what Banks (2001) calls superordinate groups where students from even profoundly different backgrounds can find common goals in which they might join together despite their differences. Sports teams, choirs, and individual classrooms can all be framed in this way so as to help students both celebrate their differences and come to understand what is universally true about the human condition while in pursuit of common aims. Banks notes that the coming together for common purposes is only possible when teachers help reframe subject matter from the perspective of traditionally marginalized groups so that their experiences can be brought from the fringe to the center of the curriculum. In this way, students from a variety of backgrounds can come to understand how knowledge is socially constructed, by whom, and for what purposes (Banks et al., 2001).

While Banks' essential principles serve as a promising guide to the current and future development of powerful multicultural schools in our nation, there already has been considerable success in reforming small urban schools. Deborah Meier, best known for the work that she has done in New York City's East Harlem district, is currently the principal of the Mission Hill Elementary School in Roxbury, Massachusetts. Like East Harlem, the Roxbury section of Boston offers educators the complex and challenging task of improving student achievement within the context of urban poverty and increasing diversity (Meier, 2000).

In New York, Meier succeeded in developing a democratic school environment by making use of the social capital that existed in the school and community. Parents were encouraged to play a vocal role in the education of their children. Teachers were involved in site-based management, and students were challenged to engage in active learning activities. Her strategy was simple. Meier (2000) contends that for human learning to be enduring, it "requires engagement of learners on their own behalf and rests on the relationships that develop between schools and their communities, between teachers and their schools, and the individual learner and what is to be learned" (p.19).

At Mission Hill, the tradition of alternative approaches to instruction posited within a community of learners continues. Mission Hill invented its own standards and new teachers can, too.

Classroom Culture and Ethnic Culture: A Dynamic Relationship

Looking at Two Ethnic Groups: Vietnamese and Navajo

Many books that address the teaching of different ethnic groups describe Vietnamese (and in general Asian) children as being quiet, submissive, and reluctant to speak publicly,

TABLE 9.1:	Myths	
Ethnicity	**Learning Style**	**Implications for Teaching**
Asian	*Quiet, submissive, obedient, prefer not to call attention to themselves, prefer to work independently, reluctant to engage in "free discussion," prefer not to partake in brainstorming exercises.*	*Didactic methods important, teachers should transmit information, strategies, etc. through lecture. Teachers should understand if student does not ask question, is reluctant to challenge assumptions/methods of teacher, or otherwise appears unengaged.*
Navajo	*Nonanalytical, nonverbal, visual learners, "doers" rather than "talkers" (McCarty, Lynch, Wallace & Benally 1991), may consider it rude to disagree in public, or not worth the risk of hurting someone's feelings by stating an opinion in class, often slow to respond verbally.*	*Teachers should employ "right hemisphere" approaches, emphasizing dance, art, and music. Teachers should employ a lot of wait time after questions. Try to avoid asking direct questions that put students on the spot.*

and Navajo children as being nonverbal, nonanalytical, and even disengaged. Review the myths in Table 9.1, but be advised: It is detrimental to the learning health of your students.

In Traditional Classrooms

The traits described in Table 9.1 appear primarily when the diverse classroom is one where the teacher dispenses knowledge. In these classrooms, teachers of minority students spend more time talking than do teachers of white children; thus, minority children "spend considerably more time listening than being heard" (Moran in McCarty, Lynch, Wallace, & Benally, 1991, p. 54). When communication is controlled by the teacher, when students are singled out to answer direct questions about subjects "for which they have little background knowledge" (Collier, Laatsch, & Ferrero, 1972, p. 70) this very classroom culture reinforces submissiveness and makes certain minority groups appear, as groups, to be nonverbal, nonanalytical, or disengaged.

In Constructivist Classrooms

The situation is different in constructivist classrooms. Where

teachers and students share talk, where the expression of students' ideas is sought and clearly valued, where curricular content meaningfully incorporates the students' social environment, and where students use their cultural and linguistic resources to solve new problems, Native American students respond eagerly and quite verbally to questioning, even in their second language (McCarty et al., 1991, p. 53).

According to Steinberg (1996), Asian students outperform *all* other groups (including whites) on measures of school performance. They earn higher grades, do more homework, cut class less often, and report less mind wandering. One of Steinberg's most striking findings, however, is that compared to all other ethnic groups, Asians so frequently "turn to each other for academic assistance and consultation" (p. 47). They collaborate, they work in groups, they pose questions, and they work on them together. This is hardly what one would expect based on Table 9.1, which characterizes Asians as independent, passive, and reluctant to ask questions.

In a study by McCarty and colleagues (1991), the use of a pilot curriculum that emphasized open-ended questioning, collaborative group work, and student-directed learning (not exactly the approach suggested in Table 9.1) was shown to enhance student engagement, content mastery, and analytic reasoning in Navajo youth. As suggested in Table 9.1, this approach was widely considered to be antithetical to the Navajo learning style. As Au pointed out (in McCarty et al., 1991), "Native American children may in no way be characterized as nonverbal . . . though . . . there are settings in which they may appear so" (p. 53). Unfortunately, these settings continue to be our classrooms.

Others have noted that a focus on the ways in which students do not fit into traditional classrooms (in addition to putting system and teacher needs ahead of student needs) converts such cultural biases into harmful, stigmatizing labels.

For example as Locust has noted (in Turnbull et al., 1995, p. 15):

Only when formal education came to the Indian Nations were labels supplied to the differences between children. Public Law 94–142 . . . caused multitudes of children to be labeled mentally retarded or learning disabled who up until that time were not considered handicapped in their cultures.

Two Approaches

Let's turn to a more practical example of these points. Think about the assumptions that inform and guide the different educational approaches presented below:

Approach 1: Monday through Thursday, a 10th-grade biology teacher presents a 40-minute lecture each afternoon on the digestive system of sheep, their eating habits, and their grazing preferences. When a student asks a question about the content during the lectures, the teacher provides the answer. If the teacher poses a question to which a student responds incorrectly, the teacher provides the right answer or turns to another student until she gets the correct response. She then moves on. On Friday, she gives a multiple-choice test based on the information covered during the week. Her evaluation of a student's learning is based on the student's test score. Although she may never return to the subject of sheep for the remainder of the year, the teacher is confident that a high score indicates that a student has learned the material and that she has adequately *covered* the content.

Approach 2: Monday through Thursday, an elder Navajo sheep herder spends 40 minutes with tribal children each afternoon listening to their questions about sheep, their eating habits, and their grazing preferences. When a child asks a question, the elder replies, "What do you think?" and continues to encourage further observation and inquiry (McCarty et al., 1991). On Friday, the elder asks the children to herd the sheep without him, to rely on one another, and to return prepared to demonstrate what they have learned. Gradually, children become responsible for the herding of sheep. Their mastery of the content information is continuously tied to, and used as a foundation for, subsequent learning.

Though fictional and time-compressed, these scenarios encapsulate much of what we know about the importance of a constructivist perspective in diverse classroom settings: Children, regardless of their cultural heritage, are curious, active explorers and constructors of their worlds. Navajo children, however, may not appear so inclined in Approach 1—in fact, they typically are characterized (as noted in Table 9.1) as passive and disengaged.

Yet, as McCarty and colleagues (1991) demonstrated, in educational settings that encourage children to tie new content to their own experience, that are conducive to give-and-take, and that facilitate exploration and experimentation, Navajo children are active learners who pose questions, make hypotheses, and draw conclusions based on their own analyses. Traditional classroom settings may reinforce not only submissiveness in many cultures, but dependence as well. If you believe that children in Approach 2 know and will remember more about sheep than children in Approach 1, this suggests that a reasonable goal would be to set up your classroom in ways that encourage questioning, experimentation, and collaboration (with or without live sheep).

TOUGH QUESTIONS:

- *Given the projected increases in the number of Spanish-speaking students, should learning Spanish be required of all new teachers? Why or why not?*

- *Should students learn about cultural diversity issues even if they live in regions of the country that are fairly homogeneous? If so, given the lack of diversity in the area, what would be the context for learning?*

?
- *Should the makeup of your classroom, school, or district have some bearing on curriculum requirements? That is, should schools emphasize more of an international perspective when establishing standards for the study of literature, art, history, and other subjects, or should we continue to focus on the contributions of Europeans and North Americans?*

- *What will you do if, like Susan Jackson, you get a new teaching job and have trouble with teacher difference? How will you resolve conflicts?*

Inclusion: Rejecting Instruction that Disables

In 1997, when her world was still fresh and ripe with possibility, Bruce's six-year-old daughter Rachel ran off the school bus one windy October afternoon waving a single sheet of paper high over her head. "I have homework! I have homework!" she shouted excitedly. Now, seven years later, her delight in school learning has been replaced with ennui, languor, and a precocious world-weariness about formal education. Rachel's school narrative lumbers forward, plodding predictably to its tedious, anticlimactic finish. But, she will survive. Unfortunately for students with disabilities, their school stories are considerably less sanguine, even for the fewer than half that finish high school. And, what of students who are gifted and talented?

If you've read this far into the book, you're probably feeling as if you need no further justification to build your instruction around constructivism. In this chapter, we're going to try to convince you otherwise because students who don't fit the mold, for whatever reasons, need good teachers who understand that the *questions students ask* are the most central issue to knowledge construction and active engagement. You already know that teachers who simply deliver information, or provide all of the questions without ever turning to student-developed inquiries (even if the teacher-created questions are interesting), will invariably face students who are unmotivated, disengaged, and perhaps even hostile. For students with disabilities and other learning differences, the stakes are even higher and the need more urgent.

Sham Inquiry

As noted in previous chapters, in spite of the avalanche of both anecdotal and empirical reports (Capraro, 2001; Cole & McGuire, 2004; Fraser & Spinner, 2002; Thomason, 2003; Marlowe & Page, 1998) concerning the positive results of progressive, inquiry-based learning, passive traditional practices appear firmly entrenched (Goodlad, 1984; Cuban, 1990, 2001; Apple, 2001). In fact, the repertoire of most teachers continues to be limited strictly to the familiar cycle of information transmission and evaluation.

More chillingly, there is a relatively new trend taking place in our schools, one that arose, ostensibly, to counter the perception of teacher over-reliance on *talk and chalk*. And it is this trend that, perhaps more than any other reason, accounts for the scarcity of constructivist pedagogy in our classrooms. For lack of a better term, we refer to it simply as *sham inquiry*—that is, teaching practices that look like inquiry, sound like inquiry, but on closer inspection are revealed to be just as unhealthy to student learning as a steady, uniform diet of teacher telling. In its various guises, sham inquiry gives no one solace but the teacher, who, thinking she has reformed her practice, continues to ignore, discount, or put aside the questions *students ask* in favor of those she believes are more valuable.

At the root of sham inquiry is the fundamental misunderstanding that constructivism is largely about what teachers do, as opposed to what their students do. From at least the time of Dewey, progressive educational movements have always been co-opted by a large set of players who, historically, have viewed teachers simply as technicians. In an effort to codify good practice, school administrators, teacher education programs, state licensing agencies, professional developers, and textbook publishers have become overly preoccupied with the *how to,* often producing scripted materials, teacher prompts, protocols, and other programmed forms of instruction— what Ohanian (in Canestrari & Marlowe, 2004, p. 112) refers to as "Stir and Serve Recipes for Teaching." Such approaches are based on the erroneous assumption that all students can learn from the same materials, classroom instructional techniques and modes of evaluation. Nowhere is this sort of sham inquiry more prevalent than in its use with students with disabilities and other learning differences. This appears to be true for two separate but related reasons: First, the predominance of low expectations by teachers of low-achieving students (particularly those who are African-American and Latino); and second, a fix which is worse than the problem: "teaching styles that stress drill, practice, and other mind-numbing strategies" based on the mistaken belief that "such children lack ability." (Berliner & Biddle in Kohn, 1999, p. 99)

TOUGH QUESTION:

? *Why are students with disabilities less likely to have constructivist learning experiences than nondisabled students? Is this justifiable?*

Sham Inquiry in Practice

. . . inquiry is the way people learn when they're left alone. (Suchman, 1966, p. 2)

Consider Jonah, a highly gifted fifth-grade student in a mixed-ability classroom. His school story captures the need for constructivist classrooms, as well as the seduction and danger of sham inquiry. Jonah's teacher, Mr. Stevens—young, energetic, charismatic—began his review of fractions and their relationships one Friday by passing out a variety of materials to each of the cooperative groups he had previously established: poster board, empty egg cartons, calculators, construction paper, markers, scissors. He asked simply, "Using the strategies we have talked about all week, please demonstrate that three-fourths is greater than two-thirds." As Mr. Stevens circled the room, checking for understanding and periodically asking probing questions to individual groups about their work, the students attacked the problem with vigor, applying what they had been taught during the last four days. They divided the fractions (in order to compare the decimal amounts), filled the egg cartons, drew pie charts, and found common denominators. Mr. Stevens was thrilled that the students seemed to remember everything he had *covered* and as he made the rounds, he expressed his pride in them with great enthusiasm.

Jonah sat pensively, immobile.

While his group was busy pasting their work onto the poster board, he seemed to just stare at the numbers. And then, 15 minutes after the activity had begun, he said to Mr. Stevens, "I just noticed something. . . . That's *so* cool. Look, Mr. Stevens, if you multiply from the bottom-up and across like this:

$$\frac{3}{4} \diagdown \!\!\!\!\! \diagup \frac{2}{3}$$

you get 9 on the left side and 8 on the right side. That's *really* cool. Is that a way to show that three-fourths is greater than two-thirds? I mean will this always work? I think it will, but I'm not sure I really get it yet. Why does this work? I think I can figure it out. Can I work on this instead? Can I?" Uncertain of where Jonah was going, and nervous about his taking of such a divergent path, Mr. Stevens reminded Jonah that he was to use the strategies he had taught the class during the week. Mr. Stevens pointed out that there was no evidence that Jonah had done any work at all. Besides, Mr. Stevens had no idea if Jonah was on to something or not.

In the span of 15 minutes, Mr. Stevens communicated several potent lessons to Jonah; lessons that distinguish sham inquiry from a true constructivist classroom and underscore the need for real inquiry for students with learning differences. Mr. Stevens believes, mistakenly, that his classroom provides opportunities for all students to engage in constructivist activities.

But, here is what Jonah learned:

1. It is more important that I answer my teacher's questions than my own.

2. Independent thinking and problem solving is not to be pursued, unless my teacher understands it and/or it conforms to teacher-approved methods and strategies.

3. It is very important that I move at the same pace and produce the same products as my peers.

4. And, my understanding can only be demonstrated by repeating back what has been transmitted and nothing more.

There is another, subtler message often embedded in practices that masquerade as constructivism as well, a message to which Mr. Stevens probably does not ascribe. The message, delivered inadvertently, but powerfully through his words and actions, is that memorization is more important than deep understanding; that activity, simply for the sake of activity, leads to greater comprehension than deep reflection and inquiry. To wit, teacher-directed activities often sabotage real inquiry. As Sewall (2000) has noted:

> *Activity based learning is vain. . . . At rock bottom, projects and activities provide mere entertainment. Teachers . . . seek to fill dead time in the classroom. Projects and activities keep kids occupied and unmutinous.*

TOUGH QUESTION:

? *When is activity learning in vain and when is it not?*

Clearly, Jonah is a remarkably bright and unusually perceptive student. Yet, there is something all too familiar about his developing school story, a story that most of us remember from our own school experiences, or see in our children, or, worse, watch unfold on the faces of our students.

Many students are essentially teacher-proof; they will survive years of bad schooling relatively unscathed. Students like Jonah, however, and those with a myriad of other learning differences, often get trampled in school. As noted above, although constructivist educational practices clearly benefit all students, its implementation is considerably more urgent for our students who learn differently than their peers. That is, while the implications of poor instruction for most students' learning is relatively benign, the relationship between such traditional notions of teaching and learning and the outcomes for students with exceptionalities is much more dire. And, because special education law now requires that students with disabilities be educated with their nondisabled peers to the maximum extent appropriate (i.e., in the least restrictive environment), all teachers, regardless of their politics about inclusion, must assume responsibility for the learning of all students.

Full Inclusion Is Changing Classrooms

For the last 20 years, most special education students received a large part of their education in public schools—but on a *pull-out* basis. Most still do. That is, students leave their regular classrooms for part or all of the day to work with a special education teacher or aide in a resource room on individual academic skills or behavioral goals; however, including students with disabilities in regular classrooms for most or all of their day (regardless of the severity of their disability) has become increasingly popular around the nation and about 80% of students with disabilities spend at least some of their day in a regular classroom. (That means they are in *your* classroom.) This change in thinking has been variously described as the *full inclusion* or *mainstreaming* movement. Several persuasive arguments have driven this change. For example, special education is prohibitively expensive, stigmatizes students, fragments instruction, and contributes to a high drop-out rate.

Although research shows (Henley, Ramsey, & Algozzine, 1993; Giangreco et al., 2004) that special-needs students appear to do better in regular classrooms than in special education settings, recent surveys indicate that most teachers are still uncomfortable with special education students in their classrooms because they feel that they do not have the proper training to work with students with disabilities. Are these fears justified? Perhaps, but in some sense, this appears irrelevant because virtually every public school classroom (K–12) has at least one student with a disability; teachers must learn to adjust to mainstreaming, regardless of their politics. Still, legitimate questions remain.

TOUGH QUESTIONS:

?

- *Do students with disabilities require something regular education teachers cannot provide?*
- *What is it that special education teachers provide that is so critical to the needs of students with disabilities?*
- *What additional training do regular education teachers need to ensure that students with disabilities receive an appropriate education in their classrooms?*

What's So Special About Special Education?

As it turns out, very little. There is some good news about what works (and what does not) for students with disabilities. What we can say with certainty about what students with disabilities need is contrary to what many regular (and special) educators believe. For example, many classroom teachers operate under the assumption that only specialized training in fields like learning disabilities, mental retardation, and speech and language disorders will allow them to work effectively with disabled students in their classrooms. Similarly, many special educators believe that they are somehow uniquely qualified (by virtue of their training) to work with children with disabilities. Many assume that the magic bullet for working with students with disabilities is finding the right placements and particular academic or behavioral curricula that match the disability in question. We now know, from a variety of research, that all these assumptions are false. In fact, Ysseldyke and Algozzine (1995) have summarized these findings by noting that research in special education has **been unable to demonstrate that:**

- specific instructional practices and techniques match or work better with specific learner characteristics; research has not supported the view that children with mental retardation need X, whereas children with learning disabilities need Y;
- certain placements result in improved academic achievement; or that
- special educators are more effective in working with students with disabilities than are regular educators.

A Closer Look at Today's Classrooms

On average, public school districts formally identify between 10%–12% of their students with disabilities, and about 2%–5% of their students as gifted and talented if IQ scores are used as the sole criterion, and 15%–20% if a *talent pool* model is employed (Renzulli, 1999; Turnbull A. P., Turnbull, H. R., Shank, & Smith, 2004). At the national level, Table 10.1 provides a brief overview of who these students are and how their learning differences manifest themselves in today's classrooms.

Despite the progressive nature of special education legislation, individuals with identified disabilities, as a group, continue, as noted above, to fare quite poorly both in our schools and in their transition to adulthood. Here is some of what we know:

- Although the overall national graduation rate is approximately 88%, only about 27% of all students with disabilities leave high school with a diploma (Turnbull et al., 2004).
- The employment rates of people with disabilities is only about 32%, compared to an 81% employment rate for people without disabilities; the employment rate—either full or part time—for individuals with severe disabilities is only 19% (National Center on Education Statistics, 2003).
- Approximately two-thirds of individuals without disabilities report that they are *very satisfied* with life; only one-third of individuals with disabilities report the same level of satisfaction (Turnbull et al., 2004).
- One in five school-aged children is estimated to have reading disabilities. Eighty percent of these students who fail to make significant reading progress by the age of nine will continue to be unskilled readers in the 12th grade, if they even stay in school that long (Shaywitz, 1995).
- Juel (1988) found that about 40% of unskilled readers in the fourth grade would prefer cleaning their rooms to reading.
- Seventy-five to eighty percent of the prison population is estimated to have specific learning disabilities and/or serious emotional disturbance.

Although clearly beyond the scope of this chapter, the most recent data on independent living, wage earning, and rates of incarceration are equally bleak for individuals with disabilities. We must ask to what extent teaching approaches that focus on the transmission of information contribute to student failure, disengagement, and disenfranchisement.

TOUGH QUESTIONS:

?
- *Why is the dropout rate so high for students with disabilities?*
- *Why is academic underachievement so prevalent?*
- *Why have behavioral problems increased so dramatically?*
- *Why do students prefer cleaning their rooms to reading?*

TABLE 10.1: Brief Overview of Categories of Disabilities		
Term	**Definitions**	**% of All Students with Disabilities**
Specific Learning Disabilities	Students of average intellectual ability or higher with significant difficulty in one or more academic domain (e.g., reading).	50.5
Speech or language impairment	Students with significant difficulty in either producing language (e.g., articulation difficulty) or understanding language (e.g., following directions).	19
Mental Retardation	Students with significantly below average measured intellectual ability and age–appropriate social skills (e.g., communication, independent living, etc.).	10.8
Emotional Disabilities	Students with chronic emotional, behavioral, or interpersonal difficulties extreme enough to interfere with learning.	8.2
Other Health Impairments	Students with chronic conditions that limit strength, vitality, alertness (e.g., epilepsy, arthritis, asthma).	4.5
Multiple Disabilities	Students with more than one disability.	2
Orthopedic Impairments	Students who have limited functional use of legs, feet, arms, hands, or other body parts.	1.3
Hearing Impairments	Students with significant hearing loss in one or both ears.	1.3
Visual Impairments	Students with low vision, even when corrected.	0.46
Traumatic Brain Injury	Students who have had brain injury as the result of external force (e.g., car accident) or internal occurrence (e.g., stroke).	0.24
Deaf-blindness	Students with both significant hearing loss and low vision.	0.03
Giftedness	(% of total population)	15-20

Source: U.S. Department of Education (1999). To Assure the Free Appropriate Public Education of all Children with Disabilities: 21st Annual Report to Congress on the Implementation of the Individuals with Disabilities Education Act (p. A-2). Washington, DC: Author

Is it plausible in all (or even most) cases of student failure that students and/or their families are to blame for weak academic skills and/or behavioral problems? Goodlad (1984) and Cuban (1990) found that students spend a little more than 10% of their time in school asking questions, reading, writing, or engaged in some other form of active learning. Is there something wrong with our children, or are schools and teachers contributing to this state of affairs?

CONSIDER:

Could 5,000 reports be right in finding that no student difficulty was related to shortcomings in school practice? Or would Carnine's (1994) question about this finding ring more true:

"If 5,000 medical files of patients who failed to respond to treatment were analyzed, would there be an absence of professional shortcomings in all 5,000 cases?" (Carnine, 1994, p. 341).

Consider how this plays out for Sam, a 10th-grade student who was described simply as a *behavior problem* when we met him some years ago. Sam's school struggles began in the first grade. Since that time, he had been labeled as learning disabled, mentally retarded, emotionally disturbed, and language impaired, depending on the year he was tested and the person who did the testing. By the time Sam had reached the 10th grade, he refused to go to school and began receiving home tutoring from a man named Mr. Smith.

Mr. Smith reported that Sam was able to do a great deal more than he was led to believe by school personnel. He spoke at length about Sam's knack for fixing virtually anything mechanical (including car engines, grandfather clocks, and electric kitchen ranges), his strong ability to draw, and his memory for exactly how things looked long after he had seen them. Mr. Smith noted that Sam had difficulty expressing himself, read and wrote at about the sixth-grade level, and was extremely anxious and self-conscious about his weak academic skills. Although the primary focus of Mr. Smith's work was on helping Sam to obtain his driver's license, he indicated that he had successfully introduced academics *through the back door.* For example, Mr. Smith had structured math and physics lessons around ice fishing trips and other outdoor activities, brought car manuals to Sam's house that they read together, and communicated in writing on the computer, frequently sending e-mail messages to one another about interesting engineering and mechanically oriented Web sites.

When we met Sam at one of our homes for an evaluation, we found him to be an extremely polite, personable, and engaging adolescent. Although Sam was somewhat slow to warm up, after a brief walk outdoors and some tinkering with an old car, Sam initiated conversation easily, and rapport was established quickly. Sam struggled markedly on tests of reading and writing and on virtually all the evaluation measures that required fluent speaking skill, but he performed extremely well on measures that demanded mechanical problem solving, such as jigsaw puzzles and block designs. Sam shared with us his love of cars, information about his collection of small engines, and a small portfolio of sketches he had made of various sorts of machinery. When asked about school, Sam became sullen. He noted that teachers only asked him to do "stuff I can't." He said that students frequently teased him; that he often became so frustrated that he got involved in fights; and that he hated school and would never return.

The teachers at school were happy that Sam was receiving home tutoring—they were happy that he was no longer their problem. Most believed he was headed for the criminal justice system; others noted that it was just as well. Sam, after all, was not bright, and he had an attitude problem to boot.

Do you know Sam? What is so sad about this story is that it is not fiction, not for Sam and not for others like him whose gifts lie outside what we for too long have considered to be intelligence. What is most striking about Sam, and about so many students in our schools, is what powerful learners they can be and what enormous talents they possess. To recognize these talents, we must look beyond our limited conception that to be intelligent and to learn, one must have strong verbal and/or logical-mathematical ability. Let's look more closely at an alternative way of thinking about intelligence, then return to Sam at the end of this section.

A Table: Expanding Our Cognitive Horizons

Howard Gardner's *Frames of Mind: The Theory of Multiple Intelligences* (1983) indicates that there are at least seven, perhaps more, distinct types of human intelligences. Although he was not the first to theorize that intelligence comes in many forms, Gardner has written extensively on the ways in which an understanding of multiple intelligences, or MI, can be applied in educational settings. See Table 10.2 below.

TABLE 10.2: Types of Human Intelligences	
Intelligence	**Learner's Strengths**
Intrapersonal	*Ability to know self; ability to understand one's own strengths/weaknesses and motivations*
Interpersonal	*Ability to know others; ability to "read" social and/or political situations; ability to influence others; ability to lead and/or care for others–to be sensitive to needs of others*
Bodily-kinesthetic	*Ability to control the movement of one's body; ability to move in a graceful, highly coordinated fashion*
Musical	*Ability to produce, write, and/or appreciate music*
Spatial	*Ability to shape, perceive, design, and/or conceive visual-spatial information; ability to remember visual information*
Logical-mathematical	*Ability to manipulate numbers and symbolic information; ability to draw logical conclusions; ability to think abstractly*
Verbal-linguistic	*Ability to manipulate, create, and appreciate the rhythms of language; ability to speak, read, and/or write fluently*

EXTENDING YOUR LEARNING:

Since 1983 Gardner has proposed additional types of human intelligence. What are they? How can they be explored in your classroom?

When we think of students who are doing poorly in our classrooms, we typically focus on the things they cannot do, or we speculate about the kinds of difficulty we believe may account for their weak school performance. The MI theory allows us to reframe our thinking about student performance. It calls on us to consider what our students do well, how they learn, and what they find intrinsically interesting so that we may label their strengths, as opposed to their weaknesses.

Let's return for a minute to Sam, who has always done poorly in school. Given what we know about him, would you say it is because he lacks intelligence? Are there things Sam does well? Could you think of a way that Sam could shine in your classroom? Or do you think simply that school should not be for kids like Sam? How do we want to label students like Sam—by what they can do or what they cannot do?

Why Students With Disabilities
Need Constructivist Classrooms

Clearly, disabilities make learning and classrooms more challenging. Some disabilities may even make the learning of some things impossible. As teachers, we must create opportunities for learning that are more exciting, more enriching, and more rewarding—in short, more appealing—than the desire to clean one's room, leave school, get involved in criminal activity, or become a ward of the state.

TOUGH QUESTIONS:

?
- *How do students with disabilities learn? Is it really different from the learning of other students?*
- *Perhaps more important, shouldn't we instead be asking how can we spark their curiosity, facilitate their learning, and, perhaps most important, get out of their way as Suchman suggests above?*

These questions are extremely important for students with disabilities, as they are at increased risk of school failure, and difficult transitions to adulthood. As noted above, the high school dropout rate for students with disabilities is unacceptably high. Without a compelling reason to stay, and with little academic success and a great deal of frustration, this should come as no surprise. For many students with disabilities, school is deadly boring; it is irrelevant to their lives, needs, and interests; and for many others, it is extremely punishing as well. But the tough questions posed above are virtually never asked. Instead, teachers often assume that students with disabilities are so different, so impaired, so damaged that it is a waste of time to pursue inquiry with them. As Golfus remarks in "When Billy Broke his Head and Other Tales of Wonder" (Simpson & Golfus, 1995), many believe individuals with disabilities are just ". . . too gimped out to work."

In fact, students with disabilities, although in much more urgent need of constructivist approaches, are far less likely to receive them. The most recent research indicates that students with disabilities spend much of their day on tasks requiring little more cognitive energy than rote memorization. Worse still, many advocate for just such an approach. Consider the following, which neatly summarizes not only a very popular view of inclusion, but one about constructivism as well:

> *There are several reasons for opposing a policy of full inclusion. One reason is because full inclusion . . . makes direct, systematic instruction nearly impossible. In addition, once full inclusion is implemented, teachers are forced to change their teaching methods to more child-directed, discovery-oriented, project-based learning activities in which every student works at his or her own pace.* (Crawford, 2001)

What is shocking about Crawford's position is only his candor.

Assuming, as we do, that there is nothing wrong, and everything right, with changing one's teaching so that it *is* "more child-centered, discovery-oriented, project-based," how does one begin to develop an inquiry-based learning environment knowing that students with an enormous range of abilities and interests may populate a single classroom? With earlier caveats about following a lock-step, prescribed sequence of instructional activities in mind, we propose instead a series of *infrequently* asked questions, or IAQs, as a point of departure for setting up constructivist approaches in mixed ability classrooms. These IAQs are not simply designed to be provocative; rather, it is our hope that they will lead to careful teacher self-reflection about the importance of constructivist approaches, about the pitfalls of sham inquiry, and about the true conditions necessary for students to get excited about learning.

IAQs

1. How are constructivism and rigid, lock-step, standards-based education incompatible for students with learning differences?

The short answer to this IAQ is that rigid application of standards and constructivism can be incompatible in many, many ways—particularly for students with disabilities. Students with disabilities and/or giftedness are, by definition, different academically, emotionally, physically, or cognitively than their age peers. Thus, in some sense, they are the paradigmatic case of how standards and inquiry are often incompatible, as such students are in a nonstandard place at a nonstandard time, and will by necessity have questions that may differ from those of their peers. But this raises an even larger question: Does it make sense to assume that there is a *standard* time and place in which students are ready (to say nothing of eager) for particular kinds of content learning? Despite overwhelming evidence to the contrary, an increasing number of states seem to be making precisely this assumption as an ever-growing number of them prepare to roll out detailed sets of grade-level expectations. Yet, in a recent study by Peterson and colleagues (2002) when teachers were asked about the range of abilities of students in their class *every* teacher in the sample stated that students crossed at least five grade levels, with some teachers assessing even larger grade-level differences. Clearly, student difference is not merely a special education issue. In a very succinct summary of this problem Tomlinson (2000) notes that:

> *Students who are the same age differ in their readiness to learn, their interests, their styles of learning, their experiences, and their life circumstances. The differences in students are significant enough to make a major impact on what students need to learn, the pace at which they need to learn it, and the support they need from teachers and others to learn it well.* (p. 6)

As every alert teacher knows, what Tomlinson says is true whether one's classroom contains students with disabilities or not. What is important is that teachers think flexibly about standards and avoid the same rigid expectations for all of their students.

2. Don't students with learning differences need to learn basic skills before they engage in real inquiry?

The value of special education can be summed up as follows: What's good for the goose is necessary for the gander. That is, although all students benefit from good teachers, students with a history of academic and/or behavioral challenges (for whatever reason) need good teachers and the kind of classroom experiences supported and driven by constructivist propositions, including the proposition that student talent and ability can be key to developing knowledge. If a teacher is simply delivering information, he cannot ever deal with the infinite variety of ways of knowing and learning that students with disabilities present. To remain interested and engaged in learning, students need opportunities to discover, create, and problem solve. But, what if problem-solving skill is precisely what they lack?

Many teachers treat students with disabilities as if they have a defect that needs correcting. To fix the disability, some professionals believe that students need high levels of teacher-directed information transmission. At the other extreme, some advocate fostering student strengths (wherever they may be), following the students' leads in learning, and letting students choose whether or not to attempt to improve the academic skill areas in which they may struggle. The first approach often results in the temporary memorization of increased content knowledge. The second approach is also inappropriate because most students with disabilities demonstrate weak ability to approach tasks strategically and often have difficulty carefully monitoring their own progress. The majority of students with disabilities also do not spontaneously initiate problem-solving behaviors, and they demonstrate difficulty sustaining attention (even in areas of their interest), inhibiting impulsive responding, and remaining cognitively flexible. Many students with disabilities, therefore, need a bridge from traditional special education to inquiry-based learning experiences.

Learning in constructivist terms is simply not possible until students possess some fundamental skills; however, this does not mean students need to earn the right to engage in inquiry by demonstrating minimum competencies in reading, writing, or mathematics. The skills referred to here are not academic skills, per se. Rather, they are thinking tools based largely on the work of Meichenbaum's (1977) cognitive-behavioral approach to problem solving. These tools were initially developed to help students initiate their own learning; sustain attention for complex, multistep tasks; form hypotheses; and evaluate their own performance. Although there are many kinds of learning strategy models that have grown from this work, perhaps the easiest and most practical of these approaches is Bonnie Camp's *Think Aloud Program* (1987; 1996). The *Think Aloud Program* is designed to increase student self-control by the explicit teaching of self-talk strategies for solving a range of problems. Because many students with disabilities lack verbal mediation skills, teaching them to *think aloud* provides a bridge to help them move toward self-directed, inquiry-based learning. You can also easily incorporate this into whole-class instruction. Camp (1996) suggests that teachers introduce specific questions students can ask themselves as they set about to learn. They involve:

- identifying problems ("What am I to do? How can I find out?");
- choosing a plan or strategy ("How can I do it? What are some plans?");
- self-monitoring ("Am I using my plan?); and
- self-evaluating ("Is my plan working? How did I do? Do I need a new plan?").

When students use these questions in the context of the curriculum (and not separate from it), together with a menu of problem-solving strategies (such as brain-storming, means/ends analysis, mnemonic memory strategies, and so on), they quickly acquire a wide repertoire of powerful learning tools that can be used for real inquiry.

3. Isn't "I differentiate my instruction for students with disabilities" just a more politically palatable way to say "I use tracking within my classroom"?

In practice this is, unfortunately, almost always the case. As Peterson, Hittie, and Tamor (2002b) have noted, most of what is referred to as differentiated instruction is simply tracking within a classroom under a different name. Even well-intentioned teachers traditionally think of differentiation this way and will often group students by a single, global measure of their perceived ability; require less of students they view as below average; and create more challenging assignments for those who are facile verbally and/or mathematically. What distinguishes true differentiation from such ability grouping is largely dispositional. That is, in classrooms where instruction is truly differentiated so that all learners may engage in real inquiry, teachers believe that all learners have strengths, that a uniform lesson format for the whole class is doomed to fail, that flexible grouping strategies (see, for example, Aronson's Jigsaw Model

[Aronson & Bridgeman, 1979]) are critical for every student to succeed, and that the collaborative problem solving of authentic (i.e., student created) problems is essential to learning. Such teachers believe further that are many ways students might obtain information and demonstrate their learning.

Gardner's (1983; 1993) MI theory is one way in which teachers can adapt and modify their instruction for heterogeneous grouping. Gardner reminds us that to recognize student talents and interests, to give value to *their questions,* we must look beyond our limited conception that to be intelligent and to learn, one must have strong verbal and/or logical-mathematical ability. Indeed, failure to perform well in one of these two ways is how virtually all students with disabilities come to be identified, labeled, and ultimately thought of as *not able.* When we think of students who are doing poorly in our classrooms, we typically focus on the things they cannot do, or we speculate about the kinds of difficulty we believe may account for their weak school performance. The MI theory allows us to reframe our thinking about student performance. It calls on us to consider what our students do well, how they learn, and what they find intrinsically interesting so that we can label their strengths, as opposed to their weaknesses, and validate the types of inquiry they are most likely to pursue.

4. How can I demonstrate to my students, colleagues, and administrators that having different behavioral and academic expectations is not only necessary but also fair?

For most students who are eligible for special education service, disabilities are life-span issues. The ways in which they approach material, the challenges they face, and the compensatory strategies they use—all these things are unlikely to change over time. Many years ago, one of us was involved in a consultation with a 10th-grade chemistry teacher who complained that a hyperactive student in her class continually tapped his pencil on the lab table, disrupting her and other students. The teacher shared with us that most days ended with arguments (because the student would continue tapping moments after he was asked to stop) and an occasional angry exchange. From the teacher's point of view, it was unclear whether the tapping was a willful attempt to continually disrupt the classroom or a manifestation of a behavior out of the boy's control. Either way, the behavior had to stop. Thinking about this behavior as something that must be changed (i.e., thinking that the student must be changed) is a mindset that guarantees teacher frustration and anger, student resentment, and often feelings of inferiority and impotence in both. One way to frame this dilemma is the following: The student needs to tap, and the teacher needs a distraction-free environment. Accepting for a moment that both are in fact true needs (and that the student is not simply trying to be difficult), are these needs mutually exclusive? Of course not. Readers who already have begun to think about how we can change the environment and not the student already know this. For the rest of you, one solution to this dilemma can be found at the end of the chapter.

Unfortunately, many teachers believe that accommodating an individual student need is somehow unfair to other students.

CONSIDER:

> *As Richard Lavoie has elegantly pointed out on his well-known video about the F.A.T. city workshop (1989), it is not about the other students! Lavoie points out that a teacher who fails to accommodate a student with a disability (because she feels this is unfair to others students) uses the same logic as a teacher skilled in CPR who refuses to resuscitate a student who collapses after heart failure because there isn't time to administer CPR to all the students in her room. Obviously, all the students do not need CPR. Fairness is about need, not about ensuring all students receive the same things at the same time.*

In practical terms, this may mean that some students will need note-takers, others will need books on tape, and still others will need extended time to take tests, complete assignments, and so on. Some students will need to demonstrate their learning in writing, whereas others may demonstrate comprehension orally, in song, or through some other form of creative expression. What is important is that we remember our goal: to facilitate real learning. For some students getting out of their way is not enough; they will need support.

5. How can students with disabilities teach each other?

Ironically, perhaps one of the most powerful learning approaches for students with disabilities is to prepare, and encourage, them to teach others. We observed this (and it was dramatic) in Jan Carpenter's classroom, a teacher in a multi-age elementary school. Steve, a student with severe attentional and organizational difficulties, typically arrived unprepared for school—he rarely arrived with his books or writing utensils, had difficulty settling down for class work, and often appeared confused shortly after directions had been given. Many special educators and proponents of collaborative groups emphasize the importance of pairing students like Steve with academically advanced students who can model appropriate classroom and social behaviors. Jan chose a seemingly counterintuitive approach and paired Steve with a student whose organizational skills were weaker than his own. After a variety of interventions that often resulted in Steve becoming upset and Jan becoming frustrated, she asked Steve if he could help a student with mild autism named Maria to get organized in the morning, to keep her materials tidy, and to remember to bring her books home for homework assignments. On the first day of Steve's teaching, Steve approached Maria at the end of the school day and asked the following questions: "Maria, what do you need to do to make sure you have everything you need? How can you remember to bring these materials home? What will you do tomorrow morning to remember to bring your homework to school?" Jan's strategy worked brilliantly. Steve began to rehearse verbally the strategies and questions he needed to ask himself to become more focused, responsible, and engaged with school assignments. For the first time, Steve began to feel empowered, as if learning was something within his control. For the first time, Steve saw at first hand the value of self-questioning, of teaching, and of collaborating with another. Finally, Steve became a model for Maria, and slowly she began to learn. Who might she teach next?

MORE TOUGH QUESTIONS:

?

1. *Should all students, regardless of the severity of disability, be educated in regular classrooms? Why? Why not?*

2. *At what age, if ever, should a decision be made that a student should pursue vocational preparation instead of a more academically based education? Who should be involved in such a decision?*

3. *Is there a value to labeling students? Why? Why not?*

4. *Are certain intelligences more important for students to develop than others?*

THE PEN-TAPPING DILEMMA

A rubber pad was placed on the lab table, allowing the student to tap to his heart's content without disturbing his classmates or the teacher.

Epilogue: Redemption and Bon Voyage

Where Is Susan Jackson Now?

When we left Susan Jackson in Chapter 1, she was crying on the floor of an eighth-grade public school classroom, ready to resign. Did she? It's time to read the rest of her letter.

I asked Reggie to get the principal because I really was going to resign. There was this little part of me that wanted to stay, but there was this great, big, dinosaur-sized part of me that just wanted to run away. The principal came down, and I was a complete hysterical mess; and I just said, "I can't do this anymore. I thought I could, but I can't."

He listened to me and although he couldn't understand most of what I was saying because I was crying so hard, somehow when he was talking I stopped crying. He has that effect. He is one of those non-emotional people who always seem to be in control. I told him what Cindy, Elizabeth, and John had said, and he basically said that whatever our differences in teaching philosophy, they were right. I am not their problem. My job is to teach language arts in my room with my students. They can't trust me to pull my weight on a team project until I prove that I can do my own thing in my own room. He also said that I expected to just walk in and be part of a team. He said, "You expect to go from step 1 to step 10 without going through steps 2 through 9, and you can't." He also said that if I chose to leave, it was going to be difficult for me to find a more supportive school (yeah, right).

I still hate Cindy and Elizabeth, but Mr. Schwartz was right about the teaming thing. Some wise words. I did somehow think, without even knowing it, that I would walk in and the team thing would just sort of magically materialize. When I got home, I called my mother (I call her almost everyday, these days) and I told her what I was thinking. I was definitely in the deepest pit I have ever been in in my life. I just kept saying to her, "I don't think I can go back. Oh God, I just don't think I can go back." The flight instinct was really working overtime. She kept saying that it was my decision, and she would support me, but if I left, I was going to be totally responsible for the financial repercussions of my decision.

There was no school the next day because the roads were icy (thank God for natural disasters), so I had an extra day off to really think about what I should do. The following day, I dragged myself to school, and on the way I decided that I had to turn to the students. So I did the Eliot Wigginton thing. I said to them, "OK I spent the entire week thinking about you and the way things have been going in this class, and I don't like it. We are going to change some things here. First of all, we are going to have a discussion, and in order to do that, what needs to happen?" Someone said that people needed to raise their hands to be called on. I agreed, and of course someone blurted something out immediately, so I stopped and said, "OK, there we go. If you have a question or a comment, please raise your hand." I sat cross-legged on the table (which seemed to throw them a bit), and, by God, we had a great class discussion in all four classes. At some point in my second class discussion, we got on the topic of rewards (the students brought it up). One student said that he really liked it when teachers gave out little incentives like candy, so I said, "So, what do the rest of you think about that?"

About four students raised their hands and I called on Tanika, one of the most mature students I have. She said, "I don't think we should have to be bribed to learn. We should want to learn just because we should want to learn."

I could have kissed her.

Then about six or seven other students agreed. Joe, a student who is just kind of your average Joe, said, "I think teachers just think we won't do anything unless they give us some kind of reward, but I think we do want to learn, but sometimes we forget because we are so used to getting stuff."

Then Saul, who has an IEP [Individual Education Plan] for language, said, "Yeah, but learning is harder for some people. And I know that people make fun of me because I go to Ms. Washington (the special education aide) for extra help, but I don't care because I need the help; and maybe learning is rewarding for some of you, but it's really hard for me; and sometimes that little extra something at the end keeps me trying." He spoke with such passion and so articulately that everyone just sat there stunned for a second, and then the class applauded. They clapped for him because he had been brave enough to tell the truth and expose himself; and that was so brave. Looking back, I guess it was at that moment that I realized that I could do it—just because my students were so great.

—Susan

As our first edition went to press, you met Susan Jackson, a highly skilled, confident young teacher with big dreams and early disappointments. At that time, the excitement she felt as student voices came alive and renewed her hopes overshadowed her initial unhappiness, her conflicts with team members, and her struggle to make it happen in her classroom. Susan was at the beginning of her journey and at a major turning point. Not all, or not even most, of her issues had been settled. She still needed to work at communicating with the other teachers as well as with the students and parents. One class period can make a huge difference in the dynamics of a classroom and in the dynamics of student learning, but creating and sustaining a constructivist classroom takes continual diligence, reflection, a strong vision, and a willingness to keep trying.

Two years after Susan sent us the "I Hate" poem, she found another job at a progressive, alternative, inner city high school in a large city in New England. In this school, teachers are "facilitators." Students set up apprenticeships for themselves throughout the city and its environs in areas of their interest. As they set up their apprenticeships, they must indicate how learning standards in all discipline areas will be met. Here Susan was able to see application of contructivist theory and was able to work in the way she had envisioned in her teacher preparation program. Shorlty after beginning her job there, she sent us a letter titled "I Love".

Hi!!! How are you???

I love my job. I love my school. I love my colleagues. I love my principals. I love my kids. Its amazing. It's real. I can't believe it's real. You have to come. You won't believe it.

Love, Susan

WHERE IS SUSAN TODAY?

? *You already know where Susan is. You read about her in Chapter 7! Go back and reintroduce yourself to Marie, aka Susan.*

You have also met Jan Carpenter, Ann Lipsitt, Janette Roberts, Katy Smith, Don Mahony, and Matt Marino. Each of these teachers and hundreds more around the nation travel on different paths and arrive in different places. Like others who leave behind safe and familiar, yet deeply unsatisfying, places for more promising territories, each of these teachers travels now with high hopes, positive energy, and yes, an incomplete map. If you made it to the end of this book, it is a journey and adventure you are ready to begin as well.

Creating and Sustaining the Constructivist Classroom is meant to be a sort of compass to help you find your bearings and stay the course on what promises to be a challenging, lifelong voyage. By now, you know that there will be obstacles, detours, bumpy roads, and periodic occasions that might make you feel as if you are out of gas. Refer to this book as you need to, and remember that to sustain your thoughts, efforts, and changes, you will need to spend time reflecting, developing, and re-developing your own compass; remember also to help your students create and develop the tools they need for their own excursions. Review the challenge statements near the end of Chapter 3 and the Tough Questions throughout the book at each transition you make. We are confident that it is the journey itself that holds the key to learning for you and your students. We leave you with words from Don Christensen (personal communication, January 31, 1997), yet another teacher who has forged his own route:

You cannot motivate others, it is true, but you can inspire them; you can reach those inner thoughts and questions and touch those raw nerves and weave enough magic for you all so that the active process is engaged.

It is time for you to go and weave some magic for yourself and your students. *Bon voyage!*

TOUGH QUESTIONS:

We close this chapter and our book with some more tough questions for you to consider and debate.

1. *Did Principal Schwartz handle the situation appropriately? Was he supportive of Susan? Did he send her the right message? What else could he have done?*

2. *How can you balance factors such as individual and special student needs, predetermined curriculum requirements, time constraints, parental concerns, the need for high standardized test scores, and a myriad of other issues and still structure the classroom so students have the opportunity to discover knowledge for themselves?*

3. *If you have only 40 minutes per day (35 after attendance), have five students in each class who are on IEPs and who need extensive individual attention, face a group of parents of which half are lobbying for a back-to-the basics curriculum, have many students who will soon be taking the SATs and their parents will "kill them" if they don't score over 1,100, and are in a district that says you have to study the economic structure of Canada even though no one, including you, cares about it, how constructivist can you be?*

?

4. *How student-centered can learning be in a high school system that does not provide for or allow flexible scheduling, team teaching, and opportunities for learning outside the school's walls?*

5. *How can you provide a forum for an integrated and cohesive learning experience if you see the students for only one of the nine periods per day?*

6. *How can you get around all those rules and regulations that seem to have nothing to do with students really learning any thing, such as the grade-a-week rule, or the decree that all students will have 40 minutes of English homework every night no matter what?*

7. *How can a new teacher introduce new ideas to team members without causing friction?*

8. *How can one teacher make effective changes in a school that does not accommodate change?*

9. *What are some of the first steps a teacher could or should take before introducing changes to a class or school in order to establish the most positive environment and the best chance for change?*

References

Aiken, W. M. (1942). *The Story of the Eight-Year Study* (Vol. 1). New York: Harper & Brothers.

Apple, M. W. Comparing neo-liberal projects and inequality in education. *Comparative Education, 37*(4), 409–423.

Aronson, E., & Bridgeman, D. (1979). Jigsaw groups and the desegregated classroom: In pursuit of common goals. *Personality and Social Psychology Bulletin, 5,* 438–446.

Association for Supervision and Curriculum Development. (1995). Reinventing science education. *Curriculum Update, Summer,* 1–8.

Atwell, N. (1987). *In the middle: Writing, reading and learning with adolescents.* Upper Montclair, NJ: Bynton/Cook.

Ausubel, D. P. (1968). *Educational psychology: A cognitive view.* New York: Holt, Rinehart, & Winston.

Banks, J. A., Cookson, P., Gay, G., Hawley, W. D., Irvine, J. J., Nieto, S., et al. (2001). Diversity within unity: Essential principles for teaching and learning in a multicultural society. *Phi Delta Kappan, 83*(3), 196–203.

Barry, N. H., & Lechner, J. V. (1995). Preservice teachers' attitudes about and awareness of multicultural teaching and learning. *Teaching and Teacher Education, 11*(2), 149–161.

Beane, J. A. (1993). *A middle school curriculum: From rhetoric to reality.* Columbus, OH: National Middle School Association.

Boyer, E. L. (1983). *High school: A report on secondary education in America.* New York: Harper and Row.

Bredderman, T. (1983). Effects of activity-based elementary science on student outcomes: A quantitative synthesis. *Review of Educational Research, 53*(4), 449–518.

Brodhagen, B., Weilbacher, G., & Beane, J. (1992). Living in the future: An experiment with an integrative curriculum. *Dissemination Service on the Middle Grades, 23*(9), 1–7.

Brophy, J. (1998). *Failure syndrome students: ERIC DIGEST.* (ERIC Document Reproduction Service No: ED419625)

Bruner, J. S. (1961). The act of discovery. *Harvard Educational Review, 31*(1), 21–32.

Bruner, J. S. (1971). *The relevance of education.* New York: W. W. Norton.

Burrello, L. C., Burrello, J. M., & Wirininger, J. (1995). *A learner centered school* [video series]. Bloomington: Indiana University, Radio and Television Services.

Camp, B. W. (1987). *Think aloud games.* Starkville, MS: Think Aloud Associates.

Camp, B. W. (1996). Think aloud. *Communique: Newspaper of the National Association of School Psychologists, 24*(9), 1–7.

Campbell, H. M. (1971). *John Dewey.* New York: Twayne.

Canady, R. L., & Rettig, M. D. (1996). *Teaching in the block: Strategies for engaging active learners.* Princeton, NJ: Eye on Education.

Canestrari, A. and Marlowe, B. A. (2004). *Educational foundations: An anthology of critical readings.* Thousand Oaks, CA: Sage.

Capraro, M. M. (2001). *Defining constructivism: Its influence on the problem solving skills of students.* (ERIC Document Reproduction Service No. ED452204)

Carnegie Council on Adolescent Development. (1989). *Turning points: Preparing American youth for the 21st century.* New York: Carnegie Corporation of New York.

Carnegie Council on Adolescent Development. (2000). *Great transitions: Preparing adolescents for a new century.* New York: Carnegie Corporation of New York.

Carnine, D. (1994). Introduction to the mini series: Diverse learners and prevailing, emerging, and research-based educational approaches and their tools. *School Psychology Review, 23*(3), 341–350.

Clinchy, E. (1994). Higher education: The albatross around the neck of our public schools. *Phi Delta Kappan, 75*(10), 744–751.

Cole, B., & McGuire, M. (2004). *Young children's construction of understanding about families and citizenship using Storypath.* (ERIC Document Reproduction Service No. ED479143)

Collier, J. J., Laatsch, M., & Ferrero, P. (1972). *Film analysis of the Rough Rock Community school—phase one.* (Manuscript on file at Rough Rock, Chinle, AZ)

Commager, H. S. (1980). *The study and teaching of history.* Columbus, OH: C. E. Merrill.

Conley, D. T. (1996). Where's Waldo? The conspicuous absence of higher education from school reform and one state's response. *Phi Delta Kappan, 78*(4), 309–314.

Connell, W. F. (1980). *A history of education in the twentieth century world.* New York: Teachers College Press.

Crawford, D. B. (2001) *Full inclusion: One reason for opposition.* Retrieved January 25, 2005, from http://my.execpc.com/~presswis/inclus.html

Cuban, L. (1983). How did teachers teach, 1890–1980? *Theory into practice, 22*(3), 159–165.

Cuban, L. (1990). Reforming again, again and again. *Educational Researcher, 19*(1), 3–13.

Cuban, L. (2001). *Oversold and underused: Computers in the classroom.* Cambridge: Harvard University Press.

Cuban, L. (2004). Assessing the 20 year impact of Multiple Intelligences on schooling. *Teachers College Record, 106*(1), 140–146.

Cuban, L., Kirkpatrick, H., & Peck, C. (2001). *High access and low use of technologies in high school classrooms: Explaining an apparent paradox.* (ERIC Document Reproduction Service No: EJ648257)

Darling-Hammond, L. (1993). Reframing the school reform agenda: Developing capacity for school transformation. *Phi Delta Kappan, 74*(10), 752–761.

Dewey, J. (1916). *Democracy and education.* New York: Macmillan.

Dewey, J. (1933). *How we think.* Boston: D. C. Heath.

Dewey, J. (1970). *The way out of educational confusion.* Westport, CT: Greenwood. (Original work published 1931)

Dewey, J. (1972). *Experience and education.* New York: Collier Books. (Original work published 1938)

Digiulio, R. (2004). *Great teaching: What matters most in helping students succeed.* CA: Corwin Press.

Donmoyer, R. (1996). This issue: A focus on learning. *Educational Researcher, 25*(4), 4.

Dweck, C. (2000). *Self theories: Their role in motivation, personality, and development.* (ERIC Document Reproduction Service No: ED448913)

Education Week. (Eds.) (2004). Global links: Lessons from the world. *Education Week: Technology Counts, 23*(35), 8–9.

Ernst, F. (1953). How dangerous is John Dewey. *Atlantic Monthly, 191*(5), 59–62.

Fendel, D., Resek, D., Alper, L., & Fraser, S. (1997). *Interactive mathematics program.* Key Curriculum Press.

Fosnot, C. (1996). *Constructivism: Theory, perspectives, and practice.* New York: Teachers College Press.

Fraser, H., & Spinner, B. J. (2002). *Evaluation of an innovative mathematics program in terms of classroom environment, student attitudes, and conceptual development.* (ERIC Document Reproduction Service No: ED 464829)

Freire, P. (1974). *Pedagogy of the oppressed.* New York: Seabury.

Freire, P. (1981). *Education for critical consciousness.* New York: Continuum.

Gardner, H. (1983; 1993). *Frames of mind: The theory of multiple intelligences.* New York: Basic Books.

Giangreco, M. F., Halvorsen, A., Doyle, M. B., & Broer, S. M. (2004). Alternatives to overreliance on paraprofessionals in inclusive schools. *Journal of Special Education Leadership, 17*(2), 82–90.

Giroux, H. (1985). Teaching as transformative intellectuals. In Alan Canestrari & Bruce Marlowe (Eds.), *Educational foundations: An anthology of critical readings.* Thousand Oaks, CA: SAGE Publications.

Goodlad, J. I. (1984). *A place called school: Prospects for the future.* New York: McGraw-Hill.

Gray, P., & Chanoff, D. (1986). Democratic schooling: What happens to young people who have charge of their own education? *American Journal of Education, February,* 182–213.

Greene, K. B. (1942). Activity education. *Review of Educational Research, 12*(3), 280–288.

Hartoonian, M. (1984). *Computers and social knowledge: Opportunities and opportunity cost.* (ERIC Document Reproduction Service No. ED 247 202)

Henley, M., Ramsey, R. S., & Algozzine, R. (1993). *Characteristics of and strategies for teaching students with mild disabilities.* Boston: Allyn & Bacon.

Henley, M., Ramsey, R. S., Algozzine, R. F. (2002). *Characteristics of and strategies for teaching students with mild disabilities.* Boston: Allyn & Bacon.

Hodgkinson, H. L. (1993). The good, the bad, and the task. *Phi Delta Kappan, 84*(8), 619–623.

Hunter, M. (1982). *Mastery teaching*. (ERIC Document Reproduction Service No: ED 38045)

Juel, C. (1988). Learning to read and write: A longitudinal study of fifty-four children from first through fourth grade. *Journal of Educational Psychology, 80*(4), 437–447.

Kilpatrick, W. H. (1918). The project method. *Teachers College Record, 19*, 319–351.

Kilpatrick, W. H. (1929). *How we learn: The psychological basis of the project method*. Calcutta: Association Press.

Kilpatrick, W. H. (1969). The new adult education. In W. H. Kilpatrick (Ed.), *The educational frontier* (pp. 122–159). New York: Arno Press and The New York Times. (Original work published 1933)

Kohn, A. (1993). *Punished by rewards: The trouble with gold stars, incentive plans, A's, praise, and other bribes*. Boston: Houghton Mifflin.

Kohn, A. (1996). Grading performance assessments. *Education Update, 38*(8), 4–5.

Kohn, A. (1999). *The schools our children deserve: Moving beyond traditional classrooms and "tougher standards."* Boston: Houghton Mufflin.

Kohn, A. (2000). *The schools our children deserve: Moving beyond traditional classrooms and "tougher standards."* New York: Mariner Books.

Kohn, A. (2004). *Deadly effects of "tougher standards."* Retrieved January, 25, 2005, from www.alfiekohnorg/teaching/workshops.htm

Kugelmass, J. W. (1995). Educating children with learning disabilities in Foxfire classrooms. *Journal of Learning Disabilities, 28*(9), 545–553.

Labinowicz, E. (1980). *The Piaget primer: Thinking, learning, teaching*. Menlo Park, CA: Addison-Wesley.

Lavoie, R. (1989). *Understanding learning disabilities: Frustration, anxiety, tension, the F.A.T. city workshop* [Motion Picture]. Alexandria, CA: PBS Video.

Levin, R. J. (1987). *Technology in the curriculum*. Chelmsford, MA: Merrimack Education Center.

Levine, E., Sizer, T., & Washor, E. (2001). *One kid at a time: Big lessons from a small school*. New York: Teachers College Press.

MacInnis, C., & Hemming, H. (1995). Linking the needs of students with learning disabilities to a whole language curriculum. *Journal of Learning Disabilities, 28*(9), 535–544.

MacKenzie, A. A., & White, R. T. (1982). Fieldwork in geography and long term memory structures. *American Educational Research Journal, 19*(4), 623–632.

Marlowe, B. A. (1990). *Identifying learning disabilities in the deaf population*. Unpublished doctoral dissertation, Catholic University of America, Washington, D.C.

Marlowe, B. A., & Page, M. L. (1998). *Creating and sustaining the constructivist classroom*. Thousand Oaks, CA: Corwin Press.

Massialas, B. G., & Zevin, J. (1967). *Creative encounters in the classroom: Teaching and learning through discovery*. New York: John Wiley & Sons.

McCarty T. L., Lynch, R. H., Wallace, S., & Benally, A. (1991). Class room inquiry and Navajo learning styles: A call for reassessment. *Anthropology and Education Quarterly, 22*(1), 42–59.

McLuhan, M., & Fiore, Q. (1967). *The medium is the massage.* New York: Random House.

Meichenbaum, D. (1977). *Cognitive-Behavior Modification,* New York: Plenum Press.

Meier, D. (Ed.). (2000). *Will standards save public education?* Beacon Press: Boston.

National Academy of Sciences. (1996). *National education standards.* Washington, DC: Department of Education. (ERIC Document Reproduction Service No. ED 391 690)

National Association of Secondary School Principals. (1985). *An agenda for excellence at the middle level.* Reston, VA: National Association of Secondary School Principals.

National Association of Secondary School Principals. (1996). *Breaking ranks: Changing an American institution* (Report of the National Association of Secondary School Principals in Partnership with the Carnegie Foundation for the Advancement of Teaching in the High Schools of the 21st Century). Alexandria, VA: Association for Supervision and Curriculum Development. (ERIC Document Reproduction Service No. ED 393 205)

National Center for Education Statistics (2003). *The condition of education.* Retrieved January 25, 2005, from http://nces.ed.gov//programs/coe/

National Center for History in the Schools. (1994). *National standards for United States history: Exploring the American experience.* Los Angeles, CA: Author.

National Center for History in the Schools. (1996). *National standards for history: Basic edition.* Los Angeles, CA: Author. (ERIC Document Reproduction Service No. ED 391 690)

National Commission on Social Studies in the Schools. (1989). *Charting a course: Social studies for the 21st century: A report of the Curriculum Task Force of the National Commission on Social Studies in the Schools.* Washington, DC: Author. (ERIC Document Reproduction Service No. ED 317 450)

National Council of Social Studies. (1994). *Expectations of excellence: Curriculum standards for NCSS.* Maryland: NCSS.

National Council of Social Studies. (1997). *The national standards for social studies teachers.* Maryland: NCSS.

National Council of Teachers of English and International Reading Association. (1996). *Standards for the English language arts.* Urbana, IL: National Council of Teachers of English, and Newark, DE: International Reading Association.

National Council of Teachers of Mathematics. (1992). *Curriculum and evaluation standards for school mathematics.* Reston, VA: Author.

National Council of Teachers of Mathematics. (1995). *Assessment standards for school mathematics.* Reston, VA: Author.

National Council of Teachers of Mathematics. (2000). *Principles and standards for school mathematics.* Reston, VA: Author.

National History Day, Inc. (2004). *National History Day contest guide.* Washington, DC: Author. Retrieved January 25, 2005, from http://nationalhistoryday.org

National Research Council. (1996). *National science education standards.* Washington, DC: National Academy Press.

National Research Council. (2003). *Standards for preparation of science teachers.* Washington, DC: National Academy Press. (Also see: http://www.nsta.org/main/pdfs/NSTAstandards2003.pdf retrieved January 25, 2005.)

O'Neil, J. (1995). Teachers and technology: Potential and pitfalls. *Educational Leadership, 53*(2), 10–12.

O'Neil, J. (1996). On surfing—and steering—the net: A conversation with Clifford Stoll. *Educational Leadership, 54*(3), 12–17.

Office of Technology Assessment. (1995). *Teachers and technology: Making the connection.* Washington, DC; Government Printing Office.

Page, M. (1990). *Active learning: Historical and contemporary perspectives.* Unpublished manuscript, University of Massachusetts—Amherst. (ERIC Document Reproduction Service No. ED 338389)

Page, M. (1992). National History Day: *An ethnohistorical case study.* Unpublished doctoral dissertation, University of Massachusetts, Amherst.

Page, M. (2002). Democracy needs thinkers. *Letters: Education Week, March 27,* p. 40.

Papert, S. (1980). *Mindstorms: Children, computers, and powerful ideas.* New York: Basic Books.

Park, J., & Staresina, L. N. (2004). Tracking U.S. trends. *Education Week, 23* (35), 64–67.

Pestalozzi, J. H. (1898). *How Gertrude teaches her children* (L. E. Holland & F. C. Turner, Trans.). New York; C. E. Bardeen. (Original work published 1801)

Peterson, C., et al. (1997). *Learned helplessness: A theory for the age of personal control.* (ERIC Document Reproduction Service No: ED399474)

Peterson, M., Feen, H., Tamor, L., & Silagy, M. (2002a). *Learning well together: Lessons about connecting inclusive education to whole school improvement.* Detroit, MI: Wayne State University, Whole School Consortium.

Peterson, M., Hittie, M., & Tamor, L. (2002b). *Authentic, multi-level teaching: Teaching children with diverse academic abilities together well.* Retrieved January 25, 2005, from http://www.coe.wayne.edu/CommunityBuilding/WSC.html

Phillips, G., & Faris, R. (1977). Learning as much in different ways at an action learning high school. *Phi Delta Kappan, 59,* 133.

Piaget, J. (1971). *Biology and knowledge: An essay on the relation between organic regulations and cognitive processes.* Chicago: University of Chicago Press. (Original work published 1967)

Piaget, J. (1995). Essay on the theory of qualitative values in static sociology. In J. Piaget (Ed.), *Sociological studies* pp. 97–133. New York; Routledge. (Original work published 1941)

Plimpton, G. (1989). Graduation speech, Tabor Academy, Marion, Massachusetts.

Postman, N., & Weingartner, C. (1969). *Teaching as a subversive activity.* New York: Dell.

Puckett, J. L. (1986). *Foxfire reconsidered: A critical ethnohistory of a twenty-year experiment in progressive education.* Unpublished doctoral dissertation, University of North Carolina, Chapel Hill.

Puckett, J. L. (1989). *Foxfire reconsidered: A twenty year experiment in progressive education.* Chicago: University of Illinois Press.

Renzulli, J. S. (1999). What is this thing called giftedness, and how do we develop it? A twenty-five year perspective. *Journal for the Education of the Gifted, 23*, 3–54.

Rousseau, J. (1957). *Emile* (B. Foxley, Trans.). New York: E. P. Dutton. (Original work published 1762)

Saettler, P. (1968). *A history of instructional technology.* New York: McGraw-Hill.

Sahakian, M. L., & Sahakian, W. S. (1974). *Rousseau as educator.* New York: Twayne.

Sawyer, R. K. (2004). Creative teaching: Collaborative discussion as disciplined improvisation. *Educational Researcher, 33*(2), 12–20.

Secules, T., Cottom, C., Bray, M., & Miller, L. (1997). Creating schools for thought. *Educational Leadership, 56*(6), 56–59.

Sewell, G. T. (2000). Lost in action: Are time consuming, trivializing activities displacing the cultivation of active minds? *American Educator,* Summer, *4–9*; 42–43.

Sharan, S. (1985). Cooperative learning effects on ethnic relations and achievement in Israeli junior high school classrooms. In R. Slavin (Ed.), *Learning to cooperate, cooperating to learn* (pp. 313–344). New York: Plenum Press.

Sharan, S., & Shachar, H. (1988). *Language and learning in the cooperative classroom.* New York: Springer-Verlag.

Sharan, S., & Sharan, Y. (1989/1990). Group investigation expands cooperative learning. *Educational Leadership, 47*(4), 17–21.

Sharan, S., & Sharan, Y. (1992). *Expanding cooperative learning through group investigation.* New York: Teachers College Press.

Shaywitz, S. (1995). *Implications of the Connecticut longitudinal study.* Paper presented at Disabilities: Unifying Services Across the Lifespan, July, Johnson, VT.

Simon, P. (1973). *Kodachrome. There goes Rhymin' Simon* [Record album]. New York: Columbia.

Simpson, D. E. (Producer/Director), & Golfus, B. (Producer/Director) (1995). *When Billy broke his head . . . and other tales of wonder* [Motion picture]. Boston: Fanlight Productions.

SIMS (2003). *How much information? 2003.* CA: Author/University of California/ Berkeley. (See also: http://www.sims.berkeley.edu/research/projects/how-much-info-2003/execsum.htm retrieved January 25, 2005).

Sizer, T. (1984). Horace's compromise: *The dilemma of the American high school.* Boston: Houghton Mifflin.

Sizer, T. (1996). *Horace's hope.* Boston: Houghton Mifflin.

Slavin, R. E. (1989). Cooperative learning and student achievement. In R. Slavin (Ed.), *School and classroom organization* (pp. 129–158). Englewood Cliffs, NJ: Lawrence Erlbaum.

Sless, D. (1981). *Learning and visual communication.* London: Croom Helm.

Smilovitz, R. (1996). *If not now, when? Education not schooling.* Kearney, NE: Morris.

Smith, K. (1993). Becoming the guide on the side. *Educational Leadership, 51*(2), 35–37.

Stecker, E. (1987). *Slide showmanship.* New York: Amphoto.

Steinberg, L. (1996). *Beyond the classroom: Why school reform has failed and what parents need to do.* New York: Simon & Schuster.

Suchman, J. (1966). *Inquiry development program: Developing inquiry.* Chicago: Science Research Associates.

Thomason, J. E. (2003). *Improving bilingual student learning and thinking skills through the use of constructivist theory.* (ERIC Document Reproduction Service No. ED479390)

Tomlinson, C. A. (2000). Reconcilable differences? Standards-based teaching and differentiation. *Educational Leadership,* 7–11.

Turnbull, A. P., Turnbull, H. R., Shank, M., & Leal, D. (1995). *Exceptional lives: Special education in today's schools.* Englewood Cliffs, NJ: Prentice Hall.

Turnbull, A. P., Turnbull, H. R., Shank, M., & Smith, S. J. (2004). *Exceptional lives: Special education in today's schools.* Englewood Cliffs, NJ: Prentice Hall.

Tyler, R. (1975). Educational benchmarks in retrospect: Educational change since 1915. *Viewpoints, 51*(2), 11–30.

Walten, N. E., & Travers, R. M. (1963). Analysis and investigation of teaching methods. In N. L. Gage (Ed.), *Handbook of research on teaching* (pp. 448–505). Chicago: Rand McNally.

Washburne, C., & Raths, L. (1927). The high school achievement of children trained under the individual technique. *Elementary School Journal, 28,* 214–224.

Weil, M. L., & Murphy, J. (1982). Instruction process. In H. E. Mitzel (Ed.), *Encyclopedia of educational research* (Vol. 2, pp. 890–917). New York: Free Press.

Wigginton, E. (1985). *Sometimes a shining moment: The Foxfire experience.* New York: Anchor Press/Doubleday.

Wigginton, E. (1989). Foxfire grows up. *Harvard Educational Review, 59*(1), 24–49.

Worthen, B. R. (1968). Discovery and expository task presentation in elementary mathematics. *Journal of Educational Psychology Monograph, 59*(1).

Ysseldyke, J. E., & Algozzine, R. (1995). *Special education; A practical approach for teachers* (3rd ed.). Boston: Houghton Mifflin.

Index

**CORWIN
PRESS**

The Corwin Press logo—a raven striding across an open book—represents the union of courage and learning. Corwin Press is committed to improving education for all learners by publishing books and other professional development resources for those serving the field of K–12 education. By providing practical, hands-on materials, Corwin Press continues to carry out the promise of its motto: **"Helping Educators Do Their Work Better."**